Reading the Southern newspapers, William Still paid special attention to columns headed by a drawing of a black man with a bundle on his back. These columns contained ads for runaway slaves.

The ads named the fugitives, told the location they had escaped from, and offered a reward for their return. Often the ad included the fugitive's age, shade of skin color, and general body build. Distinctive details were mentioned: a mark on the fugitive's neck . . . a scar above the eye . . . a broken tooth. Some descriptions were so accurate that William recognized runaway slaves who came to him in Philadelphia before they told him their names or said where they were from.

A Background Note about
William Still and the Underground Railroad

Slavery arrived in America in 1619 when a Portuguese sea captain sold twenty kidnapped Africans to settlers at Jamestown, Virginia. As the country grew, so did the number of slaves—and the unease many Americans felt at seeing fellow human beings in bondage.

Rebelling against the cruel system they were trapped in, some slaves ran away. Attempts at escape could be deadly, and the chances of success were small. Most runaway slaves couldn't read or write, had never seen a map, and had little idea of the problems they would face.

Occasionally some individual would provide a fugitive with help—food, a hiding place in a barn, directions for the road ahead. Over time this scattered assistance developed into a network of support that became known as the Underground Railroad. By 1850 a well-organized branch had taken shape in Philadelphia, thanks in large part to the skill of a free-born black man named William Still. First employed as a clerk-janitor at the office of the Anti-Slavery Society, Still went on to manage operations of the Underground Railroad in Philadelphia.

Helping runaway slaves was illegal, so the people involved rarely kept records. William Still, however, interviewed the fugitives he helped and wrote down details about their former lives. Later, he published these records in a book titled *The Underground Railroad*. The fugitives Still described were resourceful and determined people, clever in devising a means of escape and willing to endure great hardship to accomplish their goal—true heroes of American history.

WILLIAM STILL
—— and the ——
UNDERGROUND RAILROAD

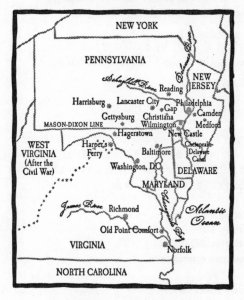

Kathleen Stevens

TP THE TOWNSEND LIBRARY

WILLIAM STILL
AND THE
UNDERGROUND RAILROAD

TP THE TOWNSEND LIBRARY

For more titles in the Townsend Library,
visit our website: www.townsendpress.com

Townsend Press, Inc.
439 Kelley Drive
West Berlin, NJ 08091
cs@townsendpress.com

ISBN-13: 978-1-59194-109-5
ISBN-10: 1-59194-109-1

Library of Congress Control Number:
2007942572

*Kathleen Stevens is a professor emeritus at
Rowan University in Glassboro, New Jersey.*

CONTENTS

WILLIAM STILL

*A Family Secret and a Dangerous Job
1821 to 1847*

On a spring day in 1844, a young black man named William Still crossed the Delaware River from New Jersey to the city of Philadelphia. He carried with him a few articles of clothing, three dollars in money, and a carefully-guarded family secret.

The secret involved William's mother.

Long before William was born, his parents, known then as Levin and Sidney Steel, were slaves on a farm on the eastern shore of Maryland. Levin and Sidney had four children, two boys and two little girls.

The man who owned the Steels passed away, and his son, Saunders Griffin, inherited his father's property—livestock, land, and slaves. Levin Steel was horrified to see that he, his wife, and their children were handed from one person to another like horses or oxen. Unwilling to continue in that condition, he told his new master he would choose to die rather than live as someone's property. Saunders Griffin realized that Levin was serious. Afraid of losing a valuable slave, he reluctantly agreed to let Levin buy his freedom.

Levin already worked long hours and hard days. Now, in every spare moment, he took on extra chores for pay. Finally he had scraped together the price of his freedom. But when Levin asked Griffin if he could buy his wife Sidney and his children out of slavery as well, the answer was no.

Levin would not accept Griffin's answer. Determined that his family would be free, Levin worked out a plan with Sidney. At the right moment, he left Maryland and made his way north to New Jersey to find work and a place for his family. Soon after, Sidney followed, bringing along their four children, all under eight years of age.

The journey was long and difficult. Sidney and the children struggled through woods and marshes, traveling by night and hiding by day, often hungry, always fearful that they would be seized. At last they reached Levin—but their joyful reunion didn't last long. Slave catchers tracked Sidney and the children to New Jersey and dragged them back to Maryland.

Sidney's owner watched her carefully, determined not to let her escape again, but Sidney wouldn't give up. To get away a second time, she'd have to travel fast. She couldn't manage this with four children along, so Sidney made a painful decision. She would take the girls and leave the boys, older and stronger, with their grandmother.

One night, Sidney bent over her sleeping sons. Her heart bursting with sorrow, she kissed them good-bye. Then she picked up her daughters and slipped off into the darkness.

Sidney's fierce determination brought success. She and the little girls reached Levin in New Jersey. Determined to outwit slave catchers, Levin moved his family deep into the pine woods near the town of Medford and changed their last name to Still. Sidney took a different name too—now she was called Charity.

Levin and Charity Still built a new life. Levin was able to buy land for a small farm, and he and Charity had more children, eighteen in all. The youngest, born in 1821, was William. But Charity never forgot the boys she had left behind. William often saw tears glisten in his mother's eyes as she spoke of the painful night when she had set off without her sons.

Charity's past was the dangerous secret the family had to guard from outsiders. Under existing laws Charity was still a slave, and every child born to a slave mother also belonged to the mother's owner. If Saunders Griffin found out where she was, he could claim Charity and every one of the Still children.

Levin and Charity worked hard and raised their children with a strong work ethic. The children helped on the family farm and did chores for neighbors. They attended school only when rain or snow kept them from outdoor work.

Young William was eager to learn. He studied hard during the short time he spent in school and read on his own whenever he had a chance—while driving his father's oxen, peeling apples for his mother, shelling corn in front of the pine fire.

When William was twenty-one, his father died. That painful blow made William think hard about his life. Working on the farm wouldn't satisfy his hunger for education. In 1844 he set out for Philadelphia.

After growing up amid pine woods and cranberry bogs, William now found himself in a bustling city. Hackney carriages and horse-drawn cars clattered over cobbled streets. At wharves along the river, steamships from the South unloaded cargos of rice, cotton, and tobacco. Gas lamps glowed, and in some neighborhoods fine brick houses rose above marble stoops. But William quickly learned that only white people rode the horse-cars and only white people lived in those tall houses.

Slavery had been abolished in Pennsylvania, and in 1844 the city had a large population of free black people. Most occupied tiny houses crowded around sunless courtyards or along narrow alleys. Many could not read, and few could write. Blacks generally held low-level laboring jobs or worked as servants in hotels or private homes.

White people in Philadelphia held conflicting opinions about slavery. A small number vigorously opposed it, and some of those people had founded the Pennsylvania Anti-Slavery Society, an organization devoted to ridding the country of slavery. Many members of the society were white Quakers, but a number of free black men also belonged.

A second group of Philadelphians took a neutral position. Often these were people who had relatives or business connections in the South. They insisted that matters relating to slavery didn't concern the North. Southerners should decide for themselves whether slavery would be legal in their states.

A third group of white Philadelphians disliked *all* black people, slave *and* free. An ugly current of prejudice ran through Philadelphia. One visitor from England remarked that there was probably no city in the world where hatred of the black population was stronger than in the City of Brotherly Love. In 1838, just a few years before William Still came to Philadelphia, the Anti-Slavery Society had erected Pennsylvania Hall, a meeting place for discussions about the evils of slavery. Four days after Pennsylvania Hall opened, a hostile mob burned the building to the ground.

William knew he faced serious prejudice in Philadelphia, but he was convinced that honesty and determination would win him success. To start out, he took any work he could get. He carried bricks, hauled wood, served broth in an oyster-cellar, dug wells, and waited on tables in a boarding house. None of those jobs lasted. None brought books and learning into William's life.

Then a wealthy widow hired William as a house servant. She encouraged him to borrow books from her personal library. William read as much as he could—but the widow soon moved to New York, and William once again needed a job. Now he had a wife to consider. In 1847 William had married Letitia George, a skilled dressmaker who would be his loving companion for the rest of his life.

That autumn William learned of a clerk-janitor position open at the office of the Anti-Slavery Society. The salary was small, but he and Letitia liked the idea that he would work for an organization opposed to slavery.

William submitted a letter of application to James Miller McKim, the agent and corresponding secretary of the society. William wrote that he would consider it an honor to hold a position where he would be considered an intelligent being. The salary offered was small, only $3.50 per week, but William hoped he would be better rewarded in the future. William's letter concluded: "I go for liberty and improvement." He got the job, and increases in his salary soon followed.

At first, the chores weren't demanding. William kept the office clean, mailed out anti-slavery pamphlets, and prepared copies of the *Pennsylvania Freeman*, an anti-slavery newspaper, for distribution.

But McKim often had to be away attending to anti-slavery business and, in his absence, William was left in charge. As he took on more responsibilities, members of the executive committee realized that William was a highly capable person—a man of energy, intelligence, and integrity. They invited him to become involved in other work. Dangerous work.

The Anti-Slavery Society publicly opposed slavery. That role was legal, but some members went further, working secretly with the Underground Railroad to provide food, clothing, and shelter to runaway slaves. Those activities were illegal.

The Mason-Dixon Line that formed the border between Pennsylvania and Maryland also separated slave states from free states. Because Philadelphia was the first major city on the north side of the line, fugitives frequently headed for Philadelphia. At age twenty-six, William was asked to become manager of the Philadelphia branch of the Underground Railroad.

He and Letitia thought hard about the matter. William had strong reasons to say no, for he and Letitia now had a baby daughter named Caroline. If authorities found out he was helping runaway slaves, William could be fined, even sent to prison. But William remembered how fiercely his parents had struggled to break free from slavery. He and Letitia decided that he would undertake the dangerous work. Almost at once, William began to meet runaway slaves who had faced incredible challenges in order to find a way out of bondage.

❧ ❧ ❧

The following pages contain stories of fugitives William Still helped during the years leading up to the Civil War.

CHAPTER 2

WILLIAM AND ELLEN CRAFT

Southern Planter with One Arm in a Sling
1848

$\mathbf{M}$ost of the fugitives who came to Philadelphia had run away from the nearby states of Virginia, Maryland, and Delaware. Escape from the deep South was almost impossible because fugitives had to travel so far through hostile territory before reaching freedom. But right after William Still became involved with the Underground Railroad, he met a couple who had carried out such a daring escape.

≈ ≈ ≈

William and Ellen Craft lived in Macon, Georgia. Although they were married, they had two different masters. Ellen's first master was her father, the man who owned Ellen's mother. He had given Ellen to his white daughter as a wedding gift, so Ellen now worked as a house servant for her own half-sister.

Ellen's husband, William Craft, was a skilled

craftsman who had been hired out by his owner as assistant to a local cabinet maker. William liked the work, but worried about the future. To cover debts, his owner had placed a mortgage on his valuable slave. If the owner couldn't pay those debts, William would be sold.

Determined not to be separated, William and Ellen decided to run away. Ellen had light skin, so they devised a scheme that involved disguising Ellen as a white person. To finance the trip north, they would use money William had saved.

Early on the morning of December 21, William and Ellen set out for the train station. They entered separate cars, Ellen taking a seat with white passengers, William with black. Even before the Savannah-bound train left the station, disaster threatened. William saw his employer prowling the station platform peering into railway cars, obviously hunting for his missing worker. Just as the man started toward the car where William was seated, the departure bell rang. With a hiss of steam, the train jerked forward, much to William's relief.

Meanwhile, Ellen also faced a tense situation. An elderly white gentleman had taken a seat beside her. He was a friend of her owner's. In fact, he had been a dinner guest at her owner's house the previous day, and Ellen had waited on him. Ellen sat quietly through the entire trip, face turned toward the window, heart beating fast. Thanks to her elaborate disguise, the man never recognized her.

During the long trip north, William learned of a boarding house in Philadelphia owned by an abolitionist. When they arrived in the city, he and Ellen made their way to that boarding house and asked for help.

On Christmas morning 1848, William Still learned that an unexpected message had been delivered to the anti-slavery office. The message said that two runaway slaves had just arrived in Philadelphia after traveling all the way from Macon, Georgia—a journey of a thousand miles.

William and other members of the Anti-Slavery Society went to the boarding house to offer help. They were led into a private room where William saw a young Southern planter wearing a fine black suit, high-heeled boots, and a long cloak, waiting with his man-servant.

The truth was quickly revealed. The "planter" was Ellen Craft in man's clothing, and the "man-servant" was her husband William. This was the bold plan the Crafts had devised. Knowing that Ellen could pass for white, they had decided that she would travel north disguised as a sickly Southern gentleman seeking medical treatment in Philadelphia, a city known for its fine medical facilities. William would accompany her as the planter's servant.

Ellen, a skilled seamstress, had made the trousers she would wear, and William used money he had saved to buy the boots and other articles of clothing Ellen needed. They knew the white planter would be expected to sign hotel registers and other official papers along the way, and Ellen couldn't read or write. To get around that problem, Ellen wrapped her right arm in a sling. To conceal her smooth skin, Ellen wound a cloth around her face as though she suffered from a painful toothache. To reinforce the idea that the planter was ill, she also carried a cane and walked with a limp. As a final touch, she concealed her eyes behind dark green spectacles.

During the dangerous trip, Ellen intended to assume an air of aristocratic superiority. Her man-servant would take care of all details. If anyone tried to speak with Ellen, William would explain that his master was hard of hearing.

The disguise worked perfectly. Moving north by rail and steamship, William and Ellen stopped over-night at fine hotels in Charleston and Richmond. They were treated with the courtesy a Southern gentleman would expect for himself and his servant. No one they met guessed the truth.

But the biggest challenge lay ahead—the rail-road depot in Baltimore, Maryland. From Baltimore the train traveled directly to Philadelphia. Railway officials in Baltimore knew that a slave brought into the free state of Pennsylvania by his owner had the right to claim freedom. William and Ellen already had their tickets, bought earlier in Charleston, but the railroad required any black person setting off for Philadelphia to present a written statement from a well-known local citizen certifying that the individual was permitted to travel north. When William and Ellen were ready to board the train, the Baltimore agent demanded the required written document. Without it, he said, William could not continue on to Philadelphia.

It was a terrible moment. The long, difficult escape seemed about to unravel—but William refused to accept defeat. He told the agent that he had come up from Georgia with his young master and hadn't known about the rule. His master was gravely ill. It was essential that William accompany him to Philadelphia. If they were delayed, his master might die before reaching his destination.

While the agent hesitated, perplexed, the departure bell rang. Abruptly, the agent agreed to waive the regulation. William and Ellen boarded the train trying not to show the relief they felt. The last hurdle had been overcome . . . or so it seemed.

After settling Ellen in a first-class car, William made his way to the rear of the train. Exhausted by the day's events, William found a quiet spot near the baggage van and fell into a deep sleep. He was still asleep when the train chuffed to a stop on the bank of the Susquehanna River—a stop William hadn't known about.

There was no bridge to carry trains over the river so passengers and baggage had to cross by boat or ferry, then board another train. The porters didn't bother to wake William. They simply tumbled him over into the baggage van, which was about to be unhitched from the train and rolled onto a boat. William slept through it all.

Up ahead, first-class passengers had been told to leave their car and board the ferry. The night was dark and cold, and rain spattered against the windows. Ellen expected that William would come to assist her, as he always did, but William did not arrive. Worried, Ellen asked the conductor to locate him. The conductor, a Northerner with abolitionist leanings, told Ellen brusquely that he was no slave catcher. It was the slave owner's responsibility to keep track of his own property.

Ellen's concern increased. William was carrying their money, and she had their train tickets. If she and William were permanently separated, it would surely bring disaster. Unable to see any other course of action, Ellen struggled off the train and made her way onto the ferry.

Upon reaching the other side of the river, the first-class passengers boarded their cars, and the baggage van was attached to the rear of the waiting train. Still no sign of William. Ellen huddled in her seat, fearing something terrible had happened to him. Finally, the conductor relented. He hunted up William, shook him awake, and said that his master was scared half to death by his absence. William sprang to his feet and hurried forward to reassure Ellen.

When William returned to the rear of the train, he found the conductor chatting with a few other men. Aware that William could hear them, they joked that the the slave might decide to run away when he and his master reached Philadelphia. Listening to their conversation, William heard useful bits of information about the city. He also learned the name of a Philadelphia boarding house run by an abolitionist, a place where a runaway slave could be safe.

As Christmas Day dawned, William was wide awake and tense with excitement. The engine gave a shrill whistle, and lights flickered in the distance. They were approaching Philadelphia.

William hurried to Ellen's side. When the train jerked to a stop, he helped her off onto the train platform. Through all the long journey, Ellen had faced danger with resolve, keeping her courage high. Now, safe in the city that promised freedom, Ellen leaned against her husband and burst into tears.

When she was calm, William found a cab and gave the driver the address of the boarding house. There they were made welcome, and word was swiftly sent to the anti-slavery office.

William Still and his companions were delighted to hear the details of this daring trip, but they knew Southern slave owners would be enraged when they learned of the Crafts' bold escape. It wasn't safe for William and Ellen to remain in Philadelphia. Arrangements were made to send them on to Boston, where abolitionists would help them settle.

Even in a city as far north as Boston, William and Ellen Craft would still be fugitives. Slave catchers could pursue fugitives into any state, and runaway slaves had been captured and returned from Massachusetts in the past. However, none had been seized there for several years, and abolitionists had vowed that none would be taken in the future. In Boston, it was believed, William and Ellen could live their life in peace and safety.

ૐ ૐ ૐ

Slave owners insisted that black people lacked intelligence and initiative and needed a white master to take care of them. Many northerners had accepted that fiction, but Ellen and William Craft turned the idea upside down. Ellen had successfully disguised herself as an aristocratic white planter and traveled one thousand miles through hostile Southern territory. Her husband William had skillfully handled the many tense situations they faced during the long trip to Philadelphia.

In this early encounter with fugitives fleeing bondage, William Still found dramatic evidence that runaway slaves were people of courage and daring. In the years ahead, his first impression would be confirmed a hundred times over.

HENRY BOX BROWN

Shipped to Freedom
March 1849

When Henry Brown was small, his mother taught him a painful truth. "Look at the trees," she said to Henry one autumn day. The branches were bare, the leaves stripped off by the wind. His mother explained that the children of slaves could be taken from their parents as easily as leaves were torn from the trees. Henry would live to see this happen to his own children.

When he was grown, Henry's master hired him out to a Richmond tobacco factory. In Richmond, Henry met a slave named Nancy. Although they belonged to different masters, Henry and Nancy were able to marry and have children. Henry was assured by his wife's owner that the couple would be allowed to stay together.

But one day while Henry was at work, Nancy's master hustled her and the children off to the slave auction. A trader bought Henry's family and many other slaves. The trader planned to take them down to North Carolina where demand for slave labor was great and prices were high. When Henry learned what had occurred, he ran to everyone he knew who might help him save his wife and children, but he could find no one willing to assist him.

When the trader was ready to start the trip south, he marched his gang of three hundred fifty slaves along a street in Richmond. As Henry watched, filled with anguish, five wagons rolled by, carrying children. In one wagon Henry saw his oldest child. The boy called pitifully to his father, but Henry could only cry farewell. Next, adults trudged past, fastened together in coffles by ropes looped around their necks. When Nancy came in sight, Henry ran out, seized his wife's hand, and walked four miles with her. Then, bound to Richmond by the chains of his own slavery, Henry had to let her go. He watched until the line of slaves vanished from view. Horrified by the system that allowed such cruelty, Henry made up his mind to run away.

                  🐾 🐾 🐾

Henry Brown knew there were abolitionists in Philadelphia who would help a runaway slave. The problem was how to get to Philadelphia. Every ordinary means of traveling to that city seemed bound to fail. Finally Henry came up with an extraordinary idea. Boxed goods were regularly shipped from Richmond to Philadelphia. Why couldn't human freight travel the same way?

A sympathetic white man, a shoe dealer named Samuel Smith, agreed to help Henry Smith. He traveled to Philadelphia to seek support from the Anti-Slavery Society. James Miller McKim listened carefully to Smith's proposal, but he was unwilling to approve the plan, concerned that Brown might die on the way. Smith argued long and hard, finally overcoming McKim's reluctance. It was agreed that the box containing Brown could be shipped to the railway depot in Philadelphia bearing a false name and address, and someone from the Anti-Slavery Society would pick it up there.

Back in Richmond, Smith and Henry Brown built a wooden box and lined it with felt. The box was two feet eight inches deep, two feet wide, and three feet long—big enough to hold Henry but allowing no room for him to turn over or move around.

Henry wanted to establish a reason to miss work at the tobacco factory so that his absence would go unnoticed for a few days. Finding a suitable excuse proved difficult and delayed his planned departure. Finally Henry devised a painful solution. He poured over his finger caustic acid that ate through the flesh. On seeing the ugly wound, the overseer at the factory told Henry to stay home until his finger got better.

Now Henry was ready for his desperate journey. Taking along a few biscuits and a bladder filled with water, he folded himself down into the narrow box with his face close to the gimlet holes that had been bored through the wood to provide air. Samuel Smith nailed the lid shut and fastened five hoops of hickory wood around the outside. The top was marked with the false name and Philadelphia address along with a large notice: THIS SIDE UP WITH CARE. Then the box was wrestled onto a flat-bed cart and hauled off to the Adams Express office to be shipped north. Henry Brown had begun his journey to freedom.

Meanwhile, James Miller McKim and William Still were waiting in Philadelphia, filled with anxiety. If the box arrived containing a corpse, it would be a tragedy for Henry Brown and a disaster for the Anti-Slavery Society.

Henry Brown spent the next twenty-six hours in stifling darkness. The box that he rode in was transported by train, steamer, wagon, and again by train. Often it was roughly handled. Sometimes the message on top was ignored, and the box was overturned. At one point, Henry rode upside down for so long the veins in his forehead bulged and his eyes swelled until he thought they would burst from their sockets.

Earlier, Samuel Smith had sent a letter to McKim. The letter said that the box would arrive from Richmond on a certain date via the three a.m. train. Unaware that Brown's departure had been delayed, McKim hurried to the depot at half past two on that date, arriving just as freight was being unloaded from the railway cars.

Only one box looked large enough to hold a human being. McKim went close to examine it and thought to his horror that the box gave off the smell of death. He read the address on top and was relieved to learn that this was not the box he was looking for.

Where was Henry Brown?

The mystery was cleared up later that day when another message came from Richmond:

Your case of goods is shipped and will arrive tomorrow morning.

McKim was afraid that workers at the depot would be suspicious if someone from the Anti-Slavery office showed up a second time to inquire about a large box expected from Richmond. He decided that it would be safer to hire an Adams Express agent to deliver the box directly to the office.

But that presented an additional problem. Employees of Adams Express Company weren't known to be sympathetic toward runaway slaves. The delivery man might wonder why the box was going to the Anti-Slavery Society office, rather than to the address marked on the top.

McKim sought help from an abolitionist merchant named Edward Davis who often did business with Adams Express and was acquainted with some of their drivers. Davis said he knew just the driver to handle the delivery—an Irishman named Dan. "He drinks a little too much whiskey sometimes," said Davis, "but he will do anything I ask him to do, promptly and obligingly."

In order to avoid notice, McKim and Davis decided that the pick-up at the freight platform would be made before daylight. To sweeten the early-morning errand for Dan, he was promised a five-dollar gold piece.

It was still dark, the streets deserted, when Dan arrived at the office with the heavy box. William Still, James McKim, and two other supporters of the anti-slavery movement were waiting. The box was carried inside, and McKim sent Dan off with the promised five-dollar gold piece.

William locked the door, and the group of men looked with trepidation at the box. Could anyone have survived the long trip from Richmond shut up in that cramped container? James McKim rapped on the lid. "All right!" he called softly.

To the great relief of the men listening, a muffled voice called back: "All right, sir!"

Quickly, William Still and James McKim cut off the hickory loops with a saw and hatchet. When they lifted the lid, Henry Brown pulled himself upright, dripping with sweat, and extended his hand. "How do you do, gentlemen?"

It was a dramatic moment. As William and the others stammered words of welcome, Henry told them he had chosen a psalm of thanksgiving to sing if he survived the journey. "I waited patiently for the Lord," Henry began, "and He heard my prayer . . . "

Henry was taken to the nearby home of Lucretia and James Mott, prominent Quaker abolitionists. The Motts listened with satisfaction to

Henry's amazing story. Lucretia Mott provided him with food and fresh clothes, and her husband invited the weary man to stretch his cramped legs walking around in the Motts' enclosed yard. It must have seemed strange to Henry to have a white woman caring for him and a white man concerned for his comfort.

After leaving the Motts, Henry went to William Still's home. He stayed there for two days while arrangements were made for him to travel by train to Boston, where abolitionists would help him find work.

This time when he boarded the train, Henry Brown rode on a seat in a passenger car.

ِ੭a ੭a ੭a

The Richmond shoe merchant who had assisted with this daring plan was elated to hear of Henry's safe escape. Hoping the scheme might work again, Samuel Smith boxed up two other young men who were desperate to escape from slavery. Unfortunately, the plan was discovered before the boxes left Richmond, and the fugitives were dragged back to face the anger of their owners.

The fury of Southern slavers came down on Samuel Smith as well. He was arrested, tried, and imprisoned for eight years in the Virginia penitentiary. When Smith finally left prison in 1856, he traveled to Philadelphia with a woman friend who had supported him through his difficulties. The black community of Philadelphia welcomed Smith and celebrated him for his bravery. Smith and the woman who had come with him stayed at William Still's house and were married during that time. Then, with financial help from sympathetic Philadelphians, black and white, Smith and his bride departed for Western New York to start a new life together.

In New England, Henry Brown had been widely celebrated by abolitionists. At an Anti-Slavery Convention held in Boston, he was christened "Box" Brown and invited to tell his story at abolitionist meetings. Brown enjoyed appearing before the public. He created a colorful moving panorama that depicted the history of slavery, including details of his amazing escape. But Brown's life also took a less admirable turn. The North Carolina minister who now owned Brown's wife and children learned that he was in Boston. The minister sent word that he would sell Brown his family for $1,500. Incredibly, Brown was so preoccupied with his new career that he failed to pursue the offer.

In 1850, Brown left the United States for England where he became an entertainer and married a second time. In 1875, he returned to the United States and continued his public appearances. There is no record of the date or place of Henry Brown's death and no information about what happened to Nancy and the children.

CHAPTER 4

PETER FREEDMAN

William Still's Long-Lost Brother
August 1850

As the nation expanded westward, the struggle over slavery intensified. Now the government faced a volatile issue: the status of territories acquired as a result of the War with Mexico. Should these territories be admitted to the Union as slave states or free?

In December 1849 the Senate met to discuss this important matter. Pro-slavery and anti-slavery advocates argued fiercely, each determined to win the day. Finally, Henry Clay of Kentucky put forth a proposal that would give something to each side. Debate on Clay's proposal continued through the spring and into the summer of 1850. During that same summer, a stranger arrived in Philadelphia who proved to have a surprising connection to William Still.

❧ ❧ ❧

On a steamy August afternoon, William was in the office folding copies of *The Pennsylvania Freeman* when the door opened and two black men came in. William knew one, but the second—a man in his late 40s carrying a carpet-bag—was a stranger. William's friend introduced his companion as Peter Friedman. He told William that Peter was a former slave who had traveled up from the deep South and had a story to tell.

William listened attentively as Peter Friedman unfolded his sad tale. About forty-one years earlier, Peter and an older brother, both slaves at the time, had been kidnapped and carried into the deep South. Just six and eight, the boys were too young to understand what was happening. They only knew that they had been separated from their mother.

Now, some forty years later, Peter—finally free—was trying to find the family he and his brother had lost. Peter had traveled all the way up from Alabama, a distance of sixteen hundred miles. He planned to ask black churches in the city to post notices about the kidnapping, hoping some elderly person would remember the event and provide him with information.

William wanted to help, but that wasn't much information to go on. "Where were you kidnapped from?" he asked.

Peter didn't know. Not far from Philadelphia, but he couldn't name a town or even the state where his family had been kept as slaves.

"What was your brother's name?"

"Levin."

"And your parents?"

"Mother's name was Sidney, and Father's name was Levin."

Those answers startled William. Sidney and Levin had been his parents' names, and his long-lost brothers had been called Peter and Levin. Was it possible that Peter was his brother?

Cautiously William asked Peter if he remembered the name of any other person from his childhood. Peter recalled playing with the children of a white man who lived near his parents. That man, he said, was called Saunders Griffin.

Saunders Griffin was the man who had owned William's parents. Deeply shaken, William tried to gather his thoughts. He told the man who had accompanied Peter to the office that there was no need for him to wait. William would look into Peter's case as soon as he finished work, then take Peter to his house for the night. The acquaintance went off, leaving William and Peter alone together.

Concealing his agitation, William continued folding newspapers. Meanwhile, he urged Peter to tell more about his life. Peter explained that he and his brother had always wanted freedom and had longed to see their mother again. Sixteen years earlier, Levin had died. When he buried his brother, Peter had made up his mind that he would find a way out of bondage.

Peter had sought extra work and scraped together every penny he could save until he had accumulated five hundred dollars, enough to buy his freedom. But he faced another problem. Under

Alabama law, slaves weren't allowed to buy their way out of slavery.

Fortunately, a good man named Joseph Friedman agreed to help. Using Peter's money, Friedman bought Peter from his master. Afterward, Friedman secretly signed the papers that granted Peter's freedom. Determined to hunt for his lost family, Peter worked and saved until he had enough money to travel north. Because he didn't know his parents' last name, he had taken the name Peter Friedman.

William sat down beside Peter, scarcely able to control his excitement. In a voice trembling with emotion, William said that he could provide information about Peter's parents and family. "You are an own brother of mine," William told him.

Peter was stunned by this astonishing news. He listened as William recounted the painful family history. William explained to Peter why their mother had planned her second escape without telling Peter and Levin she was going away. He described the heartbreak she had felt at leaving her sons behind.

William had also figured out the truth about the "kidnapping" Peter remembered. William was sure Charity's owner was furious when he realized that Charity had slipped from his grasp a second time. The man had taken his anger out on her sons, sending the boys south with a slave trader before they could learn that their mother had escaped.

Peter was still struggling to grasp these revelations when William took him home to meet his wife. William also sent word of Peter's arrival to two of their sisters who lived in Philadelphia, and the sisters came for a joyful reunion. The next day they traveled to New Jersey to meet with their mother, nearly eighty now and living on the family farm with another son. Charity's tears flowed freely as she took into her arms the child she had left behind so long ago. If any doubts remained about Peter Friedman's identity, the sight of mother and son together erased them—Peter was the very image of Charity.

William was thrilled at his brother's return, but also deeply troubled. The Stills had guarded Charity's secret well. Almost no one outside the family was aware that Charity was a runaway slave or that her name had previously been Sidney. In the whole city of Philadelphia, only William and his two sisters could have recognized that Peter was a member of the Still family.

William saw how easily Peter might have failed in his efforts to locate his relatives. If no one had suggested that he ask for help at the anti-slavery office, or if he had arrived at a time when William wasn't there, Peter would have returned to Alabama still carrying his heavy burden of grief and loss.

By now William was deeply involved in the Underground Railroad. He knew that many fugitives changed their names after reaching freedom to make it harder for owners to track them down. Those new names would also make it difficult if friends or relatives later tried to locate people they cared about.

William imagined thousands of painful separations, loved ones lost to each other forever. The sad images pained him deeply and led him to a dangerous decision. Most people involved with the Underground Railroad kept no written notes for a good reason—information set down on paper could be used as evidence in court. Despite that risk, William resolved to record the names of fugitives arriving in Philadelphia, the location they had come from, and other details about their past lives. He would guard that information carefully. Perhaps one day his records would help other fugitives experience reunions as joyful as his family's reunion with Peter.

ào ào ào

When Peter Still came to Philadelphia, he left a wife and three children behind in slavery in Alabama. Peter desperately wanted to free his family and bring them north.

An abolitionist newspaper carried an account of Peter's story, and a white man named Seth Concklin read it. Concklin felt such sympathy for Peter that he went to William Still and James Miller McKim with an extraordinary offer. He wanted to travel down to Alabama and lead Peter's family to freedom. William and McKim warned Concklin that the plan was dangerous, but Concklin was determined to try.

The attempt began well. Concklin reached Alabama and succeeded in escaping with Peter's wife and children. The little group got as far as Indiana, but there they were captured. Seth Concklin's body was found on a river bank, hands and feet chained, skull fractured. Peter's family was returned to the slave owner.

Soon after, William received a letter from the slave owner. The man was furious. He said that Seth Concklin had "met his just reward by getting drownded." But the owner was also afraid that his slaves might find another way to escape. To avoid losing valuable property, he made an offer: "I will take 5000 for the 4 culerd people."

That sum was far more than Peter could afford, even with help from family members. Fortunately, William found a way to assist his grief-stricken brother. Thanks to William's connections in the abolitionist movement, Peter received invitations to tell his story to anti-slavery groups. Moved by Peter's poignant story, audience members made donations to help him buy his family. Slowly the rescue fund mounted up.

Four years after he reached Philadelphia, Peter was finally able to purchase his wife and children and bring them north. Peter and his family settled on a farm in New Jersey and lived there until Peter's death in 1868.

CHAPTER 5

THE FUGITIVE SLAVE ACT

Danger All Around
September 1850

The long argument over Henry Clay's proposal ended in compromise. California was admitted as a free state, while Southern slaveholders were given a strict Fugitive Slave Act. The sale of slaves in the nation's capital was ended, but ownership of slaves in Washington remained legal.

The Fugitive Slave Act reflected a curious change in Southern attitudes. Southerners had always insisted that decisions regarding slavery belonged to the states, not the federal government. Then fourteen Northern states passed personal liberty laws requiring that a slave owner pursuing a fugitive must prove in state court that his claim was legitimate.

Angered by these laws, Southerners had changed their position. Now they demanded

31

that federal authorities take charge of situations involving runaway slaves. The Fugitive Slave Act gave Southern slave owners what they wanted. It included these provisions:

- Specially appointed federal commissioners would oversee all cases involving recovery of fugitive slaves.
- If the case went to court, a federal judge would preside.
- Accused fugitives couldn't testify in their own defense.
- If the accused person was determined to be a fugitive, the commissioner would receive ten dollars. If the individual went free, the commissioner's fee was five dollars.
- All citizens, no matter how they felt about slavery, were obliged to help capture runaways.
- Any citizen who helped a fugitive escape would face heavy penalties, including fines and imprisonment.

Slave owners lost no time in taking advantage of the new law. The dramatic escape of William and Ellen Craft two years earlier still angered Southerners. In October, two slave catchers arrived in Boston planning to recapture the couple. They obtained a federal warrant for the Crafts' arrest, but before they could act, the plot was discovered. Abolitionists caused so many problems for the slave catchers that the two men fled back to Georgia.

However, the Crafts still weren't safe—federal law was on the side of the slave owners. To get the Crafts out of danger, Boston abolitionists arranged for the couple to travel to England. Other fugitives, alarmed by the Fugitive Slave, Act fled north. Within three months, between four and five thousand had crossed the border into Canada. Free blacks, as well as fugitives, were at risk. Little evidence was needed for a slaveholder to establish an ownership claim, so free black people were sometimes seized, declared to be fugitives, and taken south.

The Fugitive Slave Act caused terror among blacks, but it also aroused outrage and opposition among Northerners. Many citizens who hadn't previously opposed slavery were appalled when they saw fugitives forcibly taken from their cities and towns. Slavery in the South was one thing. Slavery made visible under Northerners' noses was something else.

One point in the Fugitive Slave Act was particularly disturbing—the provision that every citizen was required to help capture a suspected slave. Abolitionists vowed defiance. Members of the Anti-Slavery Society were alert for any hint that a slave owner was trying to carry a man or woman into bondage, and abolitionist lawyers stood ready to provide legal help. The need for action came soon.

CHAPTER 6

EUPHEMIA WILLIAMS

Prisoner in Independence Hall
February 1851

On his way to work, William Still passed a handsome brick building on Chestnut Street just a few blocks from the anti-slavery office. The building had originally served as the Pennsylvania State House. After the state government moved to Harrisburg, the building became known as Independence Hall, a name that recalled its role in the colonies' struggle against British rule.

Inside this building in 1776, the Founding Fathers had approved the Declaration of Independence. The bell hanging in the tower had called Philadelphians to the first public reading of the Declaration. On the bell was engraved this Bible passage: "Proclaim Liberty throughout all the land unto all the inhabitants thereof." Recently, abolitionists had adopted the bell as a symbol of their efforts to free the country's slaves. They called it the Liberty Bell.

A few months after passage of the Fugitive Slave Act, a terrible irony would be played out in Independence Hall. The U.S. District Court met in a room on the second floor. That court was responsible for cases involving fugitive slaves. In the same building where the freedom of this country was forged, a Southern slave owner would try to deprive a black woman of her liberty.

≈ ≈ ≈

On a cold February morning, Euphemia Williams was getting dressed in her North Philadelphia home. Suddenly several men burst in. While her six children screamed in terror, the men dragged Euphemia outside.

They hustled the helpless woman into a waiting carriage and drove to Independence Hall. Here a Maryland slave owner named William Purnell appeared before U.S. Commissioner Edward Ingraham. The slave owner stated that this woman calling herself Euphemia Williams was actually Mahala Purnell, a runaway slave who had escaped from his father twenty-two years earlier. Based on William Purnell's testimony, Euphemia Williams was charged as a fugitive from labor and locked up in the dome of Independence Hall.

News of her arrest traveled swiftly to members of the Anti-Slavery Society. At once, James McKim and Passmore Williamson, a Quaker abolitionist active in the anti-slavery movement, sought a writ of habeas corpus. That writ required a judge to hear Euphemia's

case and issue a decision without delay. Federal Judge
John Kintzing Kane set the hearing for the following
day at three o'clock.

If Euphemia Williams was to be rescued, there
was no time to waste. Judge Kane was a pro-slavery
Democrat who had made it clear that he would enforce
the Fugitive Slave Law, and the slaveholder and his lawyer had come well prepared with witnesses. Abolitionist
lawyers needed to locate people who could testify on
Euphemia's behalf. A black shoemaker named Henry
Cornish, resident of Philadelphia, agreed to help.
Henry Cornish knew Euphemia—he had first met her
some years earlier when both lived outside the city in
Chester County. Henry Cornish set off at once to seek
additional witnesses from Chester County who could
testify that Euphemia wasn't Mahala Purnell.

The next day, as the hour of the hearing approached,
a crowd filled the second-floor courtroom. Among the
onlookers were many women abolitionists angered by
the plight of this poor mother. They watched sym-
pathetically as Euphemia—a tall, heavy-set woman
wearing a turban—was escorted into the courtroom,
accompanied by five of her six children.

With Judge Kane presiding, Mr. Purnell's lawyer laid out the following case for his client: William
Purnell's father of Worcester County, Maryland, had
owned a slave known as Mahala Purnell. The slave had
run away in 1829. Recently, Purnell had received a letter from an informant in Philadelphia. The letter told
him that the slave Mahala now lived in Philadelphia and
called herself Euphemia Williams. William Purnell's
father was no longer living, and the son had inherited

his father's property. Purnell had therefore come to claim a slave who was rightfully his.

To support his claim, Purnell had brought along as witnesses two brothers who had known Mahala back in Maryland. Mr. Purnell's lawyer called those witnesses to the stand. Each swore that he recognized Euphemia as the slave Mahala.

William Purnell and his two witnesses had all made that same identification. It seemed that Euphemia Williams would have little chance against such testimony. Nevertheless, defense lawyer David Brown cross-examined the witnesses vigorously. When had they last seen Mahala? The witnesses weren't sure. Where was the letter William Purnell had received that identified Euphemia Williams as Mahala? The letter could not be produced—Purnell had burned it.

David Brown pointed out that the witnesses had testified that Mahala was sixteen or seventeen years old when she ran away. That was over twenty years ago. How, Brown demanded, could they say with such certainty that this full-grown woman was the slave girl they had known only as a teenager? Did they remember something special about Mahala's appearance?

The men admitted that they didn't. They said the slave girl had been ordinary in appearance—not especially short or tall, not overly heavy or thin. There was nothing unusual about Mahala, no distinguishing mark of any kind. Still, they insisted that they were right. One witness said, "I never saw a great deal of change in a nigger, from sixteen to thirty-five or forty." He said he was acquainted with other adult slaves from Mahala's family, and Euphemia resembled them. His brother agreed with that statement. He said Euphemia looked just like Mahala's parents, who were also owned by the Purnell family.

David Brown's sharp questioning had clearly unsettled the witnesses. They had not expected their testimony to be challenged. One of the brothers became so faint he had to leave the stand. Judge Kane decided to adjourn court and reconvene at nine o'clock the next morning.

News of the hearing had spread throughout the city's black community. On the second day, the courtroom was again packed, and an additional crowd waited outside Independence Hall. William Pierce, another abolitionist lawyer, began Euphemia's defense. He said that the claimant's witnesses were simply mistaken. Euphemia Williams couldn't possibly be Mahala Purnell. Witnesses for the defense would prove that Euphemia Williams was living in Pennsylvania at the time when Mahala Purnell was still a slave in Maryland.

Mr. Pierce called Henry Cornish to the stand, followed by a married woman named Deborah Ann Boyer. Both stated that they had known Euphemia in Chester County before the slave girl Mahala ran away from Maryland. Each had seen Euphemia often since the years in Chester County. They gave clear, detailed accounts of times, places, and events.

Henry Cornish said those recent encounters with Euphemia were important to his testimony. If he had not conversed with her during the past twenty-one years, he would not have recognized her in the court-room. "A little boy is not a man, and a growing girl is not a woman," he observed. "Age and flesh and size make a difference."

Henry Cornish and Debora Ann Boyer had been effective witnesses, their testimony strong on every point. It was obvious, however, that they wanted to help Euphemia. Henry had admitted under cross-examination that he was a "vigilant" man, a person who tried to save any individual whose liberty was in danger. Would Judge Kane accept their testimony over the sworn statements of three white men?

Mr. Pierce called the final defense witness—Sarah Gayly, also black. Sarah Gayly stated that she had first met Euphemia in Chester County in 1824, well before Mahala ran away. They had worked together at the same house, washing dishes. "I was then between twenty-three and twenty-five years old," said Sarah. "She was a strip of a girl."

William Purnell's lawyer began the cross-examination. His first question: When had Sarah Gayly last seen Euphemia Williams? Not since 1826, Sarah replied.

Clearly elated, Purnell's lawyer rose to cross-examine Sarah Gayly. David Brown had earlier made the witnesses supporting William Purnell look foolish when they swore that they recognized a woman they hadn't seen in over twenty years. Now a defense witness had made a similar statement. If Sarah Gayly hadn't seen Euphemia Williams for more than twenty years, Purnell's lawyer demanded, how could she be certain that the woman in the courtroom was the girl she had known earlier?

Sarah Gayly replied calmly: "I have reason to know her, because she has the same sort of a scar on her forehead that I have. We used to make fun of each other about the marks."

At Sarah Gayley's response, a shock of excitement ran through the crowd. Judge Kane ordered Euphemia and Sarah to approach the bench. As spectators watched intently, the judge studied the scar on Sarah Gayly's forehead. Then he asked Euphemia Williams to remove her turban. A similar scar was visible on Euphemia's forehead.

It was time for closing arguments. David Brown, speaking first, insisted that the defense had clearly established the fact that Euphemia Williams was a free person, not the runaway slave Mahala. Purnell's lawyer took a different tack. He said he was disturbed by the challenging cross-examination his witnesses had experienced. Their integrity had been challenged, and the court now faced a serious question. What kind of evidence did a slave owner need to present in order to recover his property? He suggested that the outcome of this case might reveal whether the Fugitive Slave Act recently approved by Congress would be carried out or ignored.

Those comments were clearly aimed at Judge Kane, a federal appointee expected to uphold federal law. The audience waited in tense silence for Judge Kane's response. "So long as I retain my seat on this bench," the judge said sternly, "I shall endeavor to enforce this law without reference to my own sympathies, or the sympathies and opinions of others."

Judge Kane observed that the defense witnesses had given strong, credible testimony. He was less impressed with the testimony provided by the claimant's witnesses. It seemed doubtful to him that witnesses could recognize the girl of fifteen in the woman of forty. With that, Judge Kane announced his verdict: "The prisoner is therefore discharged."

The applause that broke out in the courtroom was quickly silenced, but when Euphemia Williams emerged from Independence Hall the waiting crowd shouted for joy. Euphemia entered a carriage and was driven to the anti-slavery office for a satisfying meeting with the lawyers who had defended her. Next she was taken to a hall filled with black people where speeches were made, and an enthusiastic audience rejoiced at her release.

When Euphemia came out of the hall, the horses were unfastened from the carriage and a long rope attached. Dozens of jubilant black persons took hold of the rope. Accompanied by cheering supporters, they pulled the carriage all the way through the city, carrying Euphemia back to her home in North Philadelphia.

For those who despised slavery, this was a satisfying victory, but it included a sobering truth. The outcome of the hearing had been in doubt almost to the end. The turning point was Sarah Gayly's testimony. Euphemia had literally been saved by a scar.

Behind Sarah Gayly's startling testimony lay a secret that only a few people knew, William Still among them. While Euphemia was locked up in Independence Hall, she had been guarded by a sympathetic policeman. The policeman had noticed the scar on her forehead and realized at once the danger it presented. If Mr. Purnell's lawyer observed that mark, the policeman told Euphemia's lawyers, he might encourage his witnesses to recall that the slave Mahala had a similar scar. That striking detail would surely confirm Purnell's claim.

The lawyers agreed, and a remedy was promptly found—a turban that covered Euphemia's forehead. Meanwhile, the search for witnesses in Chester County had turned up Sarah Gayly, who knew about Euphemia's scar. Euphemia Williams wore the turban into the courtroom, and the stage was set for Sarah Gayly's dramatic revelation.

As a result of the court hearing, Euphemia Williams regained her right to live as a free person. William Purnell, however, went home to Maryland with less money than he had brought, no slave to compensate his efforts, and his reputation tarnished by the poor performance of his witnesses in federal court.

ɞ ɞ ɞ

Euphemia Williams was lucky that abolitionist lawyers had an opportunity to work on her behalf. Within six months after passage of the Fugitive Slave Act, newspapers in Chester County, Pennsylvania, reported a dozen kidnappings of free black people. These cases never came to court, and once absorbed into the slave system, the people smuggled away from Pennsylvania had almost no chance of finding their way back to freedom.

CHAPTER 7

DEFYING A MARYLAND SLAVEHOLDER

Riot at Christiana
September 1851

In 1849 four slaves ran away from a prosperous farmer in Baltimore County, Maryland. Their astonished owner, Edward Gorsuch, believed he was a generous and honorable master, and he could not imagine why any slave of his would wish to run away. The financial loss was one thing, but the blow to his pride was far worse.

Over the next two years, Gorsuch tried to locate the slaves. He was convinced that they had acted foolishly and might return of their own free will if he could only talk to them. His efforts uncovered rumors that the fugitives were living somewhere in southeast Pennsylvania. In August 1851, Gorsuch received a letter from Lancaster County sent by a man named William Padgett, whom Gorsuch had hired to look for his slaves. Padgett said he knew where the fugitives were and urged Edward Gorsuch to come and get them.

Padgett was a member of the "Gap Gang," a group that preyed on black people in the area. Members of the gang were constantly on the watch for black victims they could kidnap and sell. In their cruel pursuit, they made little distinction between free black people and fugitives.

Upon receiving Padgett's letter, Edward Gorsuch planned a trip to Pennsylvania. He would stop first in Philadelphia to seek federal warrants for his slaves. Then he would travel out to Lancaster County where his son, Dickinson, and four other friends and relatives would join him.

Black residents of Lancaster County had long been wary of kidnappers. Whether free or fugitive, black people knew that unscrupulous men like the Gap Gang regarded them as salable goods. They couldn't count on help from whites in the area. Many local whites resented the growing numbers of black people, and even those who were sympathetic weren't likely to interfere if problems arose.

When the Fugitive Slave Act was passed, a number of fugitives living in Lancaster County, including one of Gorsuch's vanished slaves, had given up the struggle and headed north to Canada. The black people who remained were determined to stand their ground. They had formed a self-defense organization headed by William Parker, a fugitive from Maryland. Parker was a tall, strongly built mulatto man

admired for his boldness and leadership abili-
ties. If holding onto freedom meant using
force, Parker and others were ready to fight.

≈ ≈ ≈

William Still and James McKim first learned
that trouble was approaching from a message left
at the anti-slavery office. The message said that federal warrants were being prepared in Philadelphia
for the arrest of fugitives living near the town of
Christiana in Lancaster County. Within a day or
two, the owner of the fugitives, Edward Gorsuch,
would travel to Christiana to recover his slaves.
Going along with him would be a deputy marshal named Henry Kline and a posse of men from
Maryland.

Opinions about slavery often produced divi-
sions within families. The message to the Anti-
Slavery Society office revealed such a split. The
man who had sent the warning about Edward
Gorsuch and the warrants was Thomas Kane, son
of the judge who had ruled in Euphemia Williams'
case. Although that case had gone against the slave
owner, Judge Kane was known to be a pro-slavery
Democrat. In contrast, his son was clearly on the
side of the fugitives.

The warrants obtained by Gorsuch had been
issued by Edward Ingraham, the same federal commissioner who had locked up Euphemia Williams,
a man whom members of the Anti-Slavery Society
had accused of an "indecent readiness" to capture
fugitive slaves. To accompany Gorsuch, Ingraham

was sending along Deputy Marshal Henry Kline, who was regarded by abolitionists as a notorious, lying slave-catcher. Clearly, this was a well-organized plot to swoop down without warning on four runaway slaves. William Still and James McKim knew that the fugitives had to be warned of the danger at once. But how could this be done?

McKim asked if William Still knew a reliable person, someone who would be trusted by the black community in Lancaster County, to carry the urgent news. Thanks to his contacts among Philadelphia blacks, William knew just the right individual—Samuel Williams, operator of a tavern called the Bolivar House. Samuel Williams had often assisted William with Underground Railroad work, and he was well acquainted with the area around Christiana.

Meanwhile, Edward Gorsuch had sent word back to Maryland telling his supporters to meet him at a tavern in Lancaster County. To avoid drawing attention, he and Kline traveled out on separate trains.

In order to conceal his real errand, Kline entered several taverns around Christiana and told people he was hunting for horse thieves. But Kline soon realized that he was being followed by Samuel Williams. Kline was aware of Williams' involvement in the Underground Railroad and guessed correctly that Williams had been sent to carry word of the federal warrants to the fugitives. Kline knew that any possibility of secrecy for the mission had now evaporated. From Sam Williams' point of view, finding the marshal in the area confirmed the truth about the kidnapping plot.

On Thursday morning, September 11, long before dawn, Marshal Kline, Edward Gorsuch, and Gorsuch's five Maryland supporters were gathered in the town of Christiana, ready for action. They set out on foot through darkness and mist for William Parker's house, where some of the escaped slaves were supposed to be staying.

In fact, seven people had spent the night inside Parker's house, two of them Gorsuch's slaves. Also in the house were William Parker, Parker's wife Eliza, Eliza's sister, the sister's husband, and another fugitive from Maryland named Abraham Johnson. The warning from Samuel Williams had reached the Parker house, and the people inside were prepared for trouble. In fact, Williams' message had sped through the entire area. Black men and women living near the Parker house, both free and fugitive, had heard the call to arms and were ready to confront the would-be kidnappers.

The Parkers' Quaker landlords, Levi Pownall and his wife Sarah, lived close by. They too had heard of the approaching confrontation, and Sarah Pownall had come to see William Parker the previous evening. True to her Quaker convictions, she had urged Parker to advise the fugitives to flee to Canada rather than resist by force. Politely but firmly, Parker refused her suggestion. Instead, he advised Sarah Pownall to tell whites in the area to stay away in order to avoid the approaching trouble.

Now the trouble had arrived. Members of the Gorsuch party stood outside the Parker house, uncertain how to proceed. Just then, a black man started down the path from the house. Upon seeing the knot of men, he dashed back inside, shouting "Kidnappers!" The white men rushed to the open doorway, but the occupants of the house had already swarmed up the narrow stairway to the second floor, taking their weapons with them.

Gorsuch's companions moved out to the corners of the house to be sure no one escaped, and Marshal Kline called through the doorway for the owner to come out. William Parker appeared at the top of the stairs. "Who are you?" Parker demanded.

Kline replied that he was a United States marshal. Unimpressed, Parker warned, "If you take another step, I'll break your neck." Kline announced that he had government warrants for the arrest of the fugitives. Even as he spoke, from upstairs came the sound of bullets being loaded into guns.

Gorsuch called to the people inside. He said he knew his slaves were in the house and urged them to return peacefully with him to Maryland, promising that they would receive no punishment. The only response was a metal object, flung hard at the two white men. Startled, they fell back.

At that point Gorsuch lost his temper. His son urged him to come away and send others to capture the slaves, but Gorsuch angrily refused. His honor had been offended, and nothing would satisfy him but the recovery of his slaves. "I will have my property or die in the attempt," Gorsuch announced.

Suddenly an unexpected sound jarred the white men—a horn blast sounded from the garret window. Parker's wife Eliza was blowing the horn as a signal to black people in the neighborhood. Blasts from the horn kept coming, further unsettling the white men, and in the midst of the din, both sides fired shots. The scattered shooting died down within minutes with no one seriously injured, but both sides now knew violence was possible.

Nevertheless, in the silence that followed, Edward Gorsuch and his friends thought the inhabitants of the house might be considering his offer. If they sent out the two fugitives, the white men reasoned, the matter would be over. Actually, those inside were stalling for time, waiting for supporters summoned by the horn to arrive.

In minutes those supporters showed up, black men and women stepping out of the cornfields, emerging from the woods, striding up the lane. Some carried guns, while others held corn cutters or scythes. Among the new arrivals was the third of Gorsuch's slaves.

Amid the growing crowd of black people, two white men also appeared. Castner Hanway, a mild-mannered miller who lived just down the road, had heard about the confrontation. He rode over on his horse to find out what was happening. A local storekeeper, Elijah Lewis, arrived on foot, walking across the fields. Lewis had been told of the trouble earlier by a black farmer who showed up as Lewis was opening his store. The agitated farmer said kidnappers had surrounded William Parker's house and pleaded with Lewis to come and see that justice was done.

When the Southerners saw the white men arrive, they believed they understood why they were facing such hostility. In their minds, black people were incapable of planning this kind of determined resistance on their own. The Southerners felt sure that the two white men were abolitionists, and the one on a horse was the leader of the mob.

Marshal Kline, on the other hand, felt relieved. He thought the white men would help him deal with the increasingly dangerous situation. He spoke at once to Castner Hanway and Elijah Lewis. As citizens, he said, they were bound by federal law to help capture fugitives. But Hanway and Lewis had no interest in helping the marshal. Their only concern in coming to Parker's house was to help avert bloodshed.

By now, more black people had appeared, between seventy-five and one hundred in all. Violence could still have been averted if the white men had chosen to withdraw, but one of Gorsuch's slaves came out of the house with a pistol in his hand and confronted his former master. He and Gorsuch exchanged angry words, and the fugitive said, "Old man, you had better go home to Maryland." Gorsuch, wild with rage and humiliation, retorted, "You had better give up, and come home with me!"

At that, the fugitive struck Gorsuch on the head, and Gorsuch fell to the ground. Immediately the situation exploded. All the injustice and mis-treatment these black people had known was now directed against this group of individuals who had come to fasten the chains of slavery around three of them. Gorsuch was clubbed again and shot multiple times. Dickinson Gorsuch, rushing to help his father, was peppered by pellets from a shotgun wielded by William Parker's brother-in-law. Events had spun out of control, and the white men realized, to their astonishment, that they were fighting for their lives.

As more shots were fired, more blows delivered, Dickinson Gorsuch, blood streaming from his mouth and side, staggered to the edge of the woods and fell down by a large stump. The other white men scrambled for safety. Elijah Lewis headed for the creek, and Henry Kline escaped into the cornfield. Castner Hanway and the remaining Southerners fled down the lane with black people behind and around them, shouting and brandishing weapons.

After the would-be kidnappers vanished, the fury of the mob subsided. The black people dispersed, knowing that white retribution would come quickly. Dickinson Gorsuch lay in the weeds, barely alive. Finally a white man, probably Parker's landlord, Levi Pownall, appeared and gave him water. The gravely wounded young man was moved to the Pownalls' house where, for days, he lay in critical condition. In the end, Dickinson Gorsuch survived, thanks, his brother later wrote, to the kindness of the Pownalls, good medical care, and God's blessing.

By the end of the day, Edward Gorsuch's other companions had found safety, but Gorsuch himself was dead. His body had been examined by the coroner in Christiana and was on its way down to Maryland on the night train.

The three slaves Gorsuch had come to recover took flight immediately after the riot. In a desperate scramble to avoid capture, they headed north and eventually reached safety. William Parker and the other two men who had been in the Parker house stayed on in the neighborhood, hiding out until darkness fell. They may have found the refuge they needed in the home of Levi and Sarah Pownall. If so, then for some time on this bloody day, Dickinson Gorsuch lay under the same roof as the black men responsible for his father's death.

Over the next two days, hiding in haystacks and barns, William Parker and his two companions managed to avoid capture. They traveled five hundred miles to Rochester, New York, partly on foot, partly by railroad and horse-drawn coach. In Rochester they sought help from a man Parker had known during his days in slavery, one of the country's most famous fugitives and anti-slavery spokesmen, Frederick Douglass.

Douglass was astonished to see the men on his doorstep but received them warmly, regarding them as heroes in the battle black Americans were waging for their freedom. However, Douglass knew their presence in his home was dangerous. New York newspapers had already carried news of the Christiana incident, with the three men identified not only as fugitives from slavery, but as suspects in the murder of a prominent white Southerner. Douglass decided to put the men on a steamboat that crossed Lake Ontario to Toronto. He conveyed the men to the waterfront landing after dark, fearful at every moment that slave-catchers might spring from the darkness. To his relief, the fugitives reached the boat safely and departed for Canada.

Meanwhile, news of the Christiana riot had brought a swift response from local and federal officials. By the following night about fifty local men and a group of enraged Southerners up from Baltimore were sworn into a posse. The mood was hostile, the newly appointed deputies hot for revenge. In a parallel move, federal officials brought about forty-five marines and forty Philadelphia policemen out from the city and turned them loose to hunt down suspects.

The searchers, both local and federal, scoured the countryside in a determined attempt to scoop up every black person and any white man suspected of involvement. Neither group was overly concerned with constitutional rights, so rough handling of suspects was common. An article in the *Pennsylvania Freeman* said people were "hunted like partridges upon the mountains."

Elijah Lewis and Castner Hanway learned that warrants had been issued for their arrest and chose to turn themselves in. By now, they were widely regarded as the leaders of the black mob and thus responsible for Edward Gorsuch's death and the escape of the slaves who had caused it. The prevailing mood was so hostile that the two men had feared they might become victims of a lynch party.

During the three days following the riot, local authorities in Christiana took testimony from area residents. Then, at the county courthouse in Lancaster City, federal prosecutors began their own hearings. The primary witnesses for the federal prosecution were Marshal Kline and a local black man named Harvey Scott, who claimed to have witnessed the battle. Scott was essential to the case because he was the only person able to identify the blacks who had participated.

Surprisingly, the federal prosecutors released all the women they had in custody, even William Parker's wife and her sister, whose husband had shot Dickinson Gorsuch. No reason was given for their action. Perhaps the prosecutors didn't believe that a jury would convict two young mothers of a capital crime. Perhaps they thought that the women were influenced by the men involved. Or perhaps they simply felt that Southern honor would not be satisfied by the punishment of two black women. At any rate, once released, the women gathered their children and safely joined their husbands in Canada.

For almost four months the grand jury deliberated. During that time, accused individuals, as well as some witnesses, were kept under lock and key in Philadelphia's Moyamensing Prison. Eventually thirty-eight men were indicted. The charge: treason, a crime punishable by death. Conviction of riot and murder alone would not satisfy wounded

Southern honor. Outrage over the riot and the violence that resulted ran too deep. Only a decision by a federal court that treason had been committed would suffice.

While those in prison were waiting for the trial to begin, William Still visited regularly, supplying whatever personal supplies anyone needed. Support came from another direction as well. A fine Thanksgiving dinner arrived at the prison—six fat turkeys and a huge pound cake, enough to provide a feast to all the prisoners and the officials guarding them. The generous donor was Thomas Kane, son of Judge John Kane and the informant who had first sent news of the warrants to the Anti-Slavery Society office. Ironically, Thomas Kane's father was one of the two justices who would now preside over the trial of these prisoners.

Castner Hanway was tried first, in proceedings that began on Monday, November 24. Presiding with Judge Kane was Robert Grier, an associate justice of the Supreme Court. Like Kane, Grier had made it clear that he would vigorously enforce the Fugitive Slave Law. As a result, the lawyers defending Hanway decided not to use the trial as a forum for attacking either the Fugitive Slave Law or the practice of slavery. Instead, they focused on rebutting the specific charge of treason, realizing that treason would be a difficult charge for the prosecution to prove.

In the lengthy, hard-fought trial, the prosecution faced an uphill battle. To convict a defendant of treason, prosecutors had to establish a chain of evidence that tightly linked the defendant to three points: the idea of committing a treasonous action, plans to carry out that action, and the actual performance of it. Castner Hanway had been present at the riot; that was all. Nothing connected him to events preceding the riot or to the direction of it.

Moreover, the prosecution's case depended heavily on their two main witnesses, Marshall Kline and Harvey Scott, and neither proved effective. Kline's unsavory reputation, plus the fact that he had changed his story several times before the trial, undercut his credibility. Even worse, Harvey Scott, the only person who knew by sight any of the black people who had participated in the mob, suddenly decided that he hadn't been present at the riot after all. He claimed authorities had earlier pressured him into saying he was there.

Eighteen days after the trial began, testimony ended. In his charge to the jury, Justice Grier stated that the evidence clearly showed that participants in this event were guilty of riot and murder. However, the charge against Castner Hanway was treason, so state courts would have to attend to those matters. On the count of treason, said Grier, the evidence was inadequate, and, in his opinion, jury members would have to acquit. The jury's verdict came back in less than fifteen minutes: Not guilty.

Later, lesser charges against the other defendants were also set aside, and the people waiting in Moyamensing Prison were released. However, defendants left the prison burdened by debts arising from their legal problems. Black supporters from as far away as Rochester, New York, paid off debts for the black prisoners while local Quakers aided Castner Hanway.

A grand jury in Lancaster took up the charges of riot and murder for the state of Pennsylvania, but the men most directly involved—Gorsuch's slaves, William Parker, and the other two men who had been in his house that fateful night—had long since escaped to Canada. Moreover, the primary witness left for the prosecution, Deputy Marshal Kline, had lost his credibility. As a result, no one was indicted.

ea ea ea

William admired the brave-hearted men and women who had resisted the slave-catchers at Christiana. "They loved liberty and hated slavery," he said, "and when the slave-catchers arrived, they were prepared for them." Many Marylanders, however, were horrified at the outcome of the trial. If the law would not avenge Gorsuch's death, some believed that they would have to seek their own justice.

CHAPTER
8

FORMATION OF THE VIGILANCE COMMITTEE

Help for the Hunted
December 1852

In some Northern cities, abolitionists had formed vigilance committees. Members of these committees watched the streets for fugitives in need of help. They listened for news that slave catchers had arrived in town seeking fugitives. When action was needed, vigilance committee members provided it.

Philadelphia had had a vigilance committee, but by 1852 it was no longer active. After passage of the Fugitive Slave Act, the need for a new committee became increasingly evident. In December 1852 James Miller McKim called a meeting at the anti-slavery office to urge formation of such a group. Those in attendance quickly selected a general committee, then a four-person acting committee with William Still as chair. The acting committee would be the nerve center of operations, efficient and able to respond quickly. In addition to William, the remaining members were two other black men and the white Quaker abolitionist Passmore Williamson.

The names and addresses of committee members were posted at once in Philadelphia's black churches. William was well known and respected in the black community, and he knew that help from blacks would be essential. The city's black people held jobs as laborers, as porters on steamboat wharves, as waiters and maids in hotels and boarding houses. As black people went about their daily routine, they noticed strangers who might be newly arrived fugitives or slave catchers in search of runaway slaves. They overheard conversations that would never reach the ears of white abolitionists. Useful information these black men and women picked up would be swiftly passed to the Vigilance Committee.

William's new role with the Vigilance Committee added to his responsibilities. Thanks to William's efficiency, the Philadelphia station of the Underground Railroad was now a well-organized operation. Northern Delaware and southern Pennsylvania were generally the first areas where runaway slaves found help from the underground. Operatives there often sent fugitives into Philadelphia by train or boat. William arranged for a guide to meet them and bring them to a safe location, often his own home. Letitia Still prepared food for the fugitives, washed and mended their clothes, and nursed those who were ill or wounded. Meanwhile, William arranged train tickets and wrote letters of introduction for fugitives to carry to underground workers at their next destination.

Late at night, when other duties were finished, William took out his record book and asked fugitives to tell him about their past. As he wrote down their stories, William often heard a fugitive say he had been "owned by" someone. "Owned by" . . . William despised that phrase. Writing it down, he often substituted a dash for the word "owned."

Should any man or woman be allowed to own another person? That issue would increasingly trouble consciences and divide citizens during the coming decade.

CHAPTER 9

WESLEY HARRIS AND THE MATTERSON BROTHERS

Betrayed!
November 1853

Most slaves who ran away were young men, physically strong and better able than women or older men to endure the hardships of the trip north. Young men were also less likely to have responsibility for children or other relatives. Wesley Harris was one young man who undertook the difficult journey. He reached Philadelphia, but his terrible experiences along the way reminded William Still of a hard truth—for many runaway slaves, the effort to escape ended not in freedom but in failure and despair.

෧෧ ෧෧ ෧෧

Wesley Harris was still weak from the gunshot wounds that had torn apart his arm a few weeks earlier, but he was determined to tell William Still about his trip north. William wrote as fast as he could, trying to capture every bitter detail of

Wesley's story.

Wesley had been born in a small Virginia town in an area that later became part of West Virginia. From boyhood, Wesley had been hired out by his owner. That was a practice common among slave-owners—send a slave out to work for someone else, then pocket most of the pay the slave received.

The previous January, Wesley had been sent to nearby Harpers Ferry to work at a hotel owned by a widow named Mrs. Carroll. Wesley spoke well of Mrs. Carroll. For a slave owner, he said, she was a kind person.

Mrs. Carroll may have been kind, but the overseer she hired to manage her slaves was just the opposite. On one occasion, angry with Wesley over some small matter, the overseer began to whip him. Wesley resisted, striking out at the overseer—a terrible offense on the part of a slave. The furious overseer sent word of the incident to Wesley's owner, and the owner wrote back, telling him how to handle this unruly slave. If Wesley refused to accept punishment in the future, the overseer was to put him in prison and sell him at once. If nothing of that sort happened, the owner planned to sell Wesley anyway the following Christmas.

The overseer showed the letter to Mrs. Carroll, and Mrs. Carroll, concerned for Wesley's future, secretly told Wesley. If he could find a way to help himself, said the widow, he should take it. That was all the encouragement Wesley needed. From that moment on, he began to think about how he could escape.

A friend of Wesley's named Craven Matterson had already decided to head north. He and Wesley decided to travel together, taking along Craven's two younger brothers. Slaves usually had a free day on Sunday, so the small group slipped away on a Saturday night, hoping they wouldn't be missed until Monday morning. They set out on foot across the rough countryside headed for Gettysburg, Pennsylvania, where it was rumored that fugitives could find help. Although slaves were not allowed to own or carry weapons, Wesley and Craven had somehow gotten hold of guns. In addition, Wesley carried a sword.

During the next two days, they traveled about sixty miles, arriving in early morning at the outskirts of a small town in Maryland close to the Pennsylvania border. There they met a friendly black man who warned them that they had entered dangerous territory. Whites in that area were hostile toward black people, he said, and they kept special watch for runaway slaves trying to escape across the border.

Alarmed, the four fugitives hid in a nearby woods. They planned to stay there till dark, but were frightened off when they heard the sound of someone splitting logs. They crept out of the woods and darted into a thicket of trees near a barn. To their dismay, a dog came sniffing through the trees and began to bark at them. Before they could escape, the farmer who owned the dog showed up.

When the farmer asked what the men were doing there, they told him the story they had invented earlier—they were free blacks, headed for

Gettysburg, Pennsylvania to visit relatives. The farmer, unconvinced, said they looked like runaway slaves. However, he spoke in a kind manner, and Wesley thought he might be a Quaker. That was reassuring, as Quakers were generally opposed to slavery.

When the farmer invited the fugitives to hide in his barn till evening, they cautiously accepted. The farmer and his daughter brought them breakfast, for which the hungry men gladly paid a dollar. Then the farmer suggested that they hide up in the hayloft till darkness fell. At that time, he would direct them onto the road to Gettysburg.

The offer was welcome to the exhausted young men, and they quickly fell asleep—all but Wesley. Wesley was troubled, sensing that something wasn't right. His fears were well founded. Around midday, Wesley heard men's voices outside the barn. He woke his companions and whispered that they had been betrayed. The barn door opened, and eight white men came in, bearing guns. As the terrified fugitives crouched in the hayloft, they heard one man ask the farmer if he had any long straw. The farmer replied that he did, and three of the white men started up into the hayloft.

When they discovered the black men huddled there, the whites acted surprised. One called to the farmer, "Are you harboring runaway Negroes in your barn?" The farmer denied any knowledge of the men in the hayloft.

The fugitives were ordered down. Facing the white men, Wesley and his friends repeated the story they had told the farmer—they were free blacks traveling to Gettysburg to visit relatives. The white men asked if they had passes. The fugitives shook their heads. Where they came from they hadn't been required to carry passes, Wesley explained. The whites exchanged glances. "Then you'll have to appear before the magistrate," they declared. If the magistrate was satisfied with their story, they could go on.

The white men produced coils of rope and prepared to tie up the fugitives. At once, Wesley saw what lay ahead—he and the Mattersons would be imprisoned, whipped, and sold to the Deep South. Anger flared inside him, and Wesley pulled out his pistol. "If you want to take me," he cried, "you'll have to kill me or cripple me first." At the same moment, Craven shouted, "Where is the man that betrayed us?" Catching sight of the farmer, Craven raised his gun and fired.

Someone seized Wesley by the shoulder, and Wesley spun around, gun cocked. The man flung up his hand, spoiling Wesley's aim, but the pistol shot burned the man's face and wounded his arm. Wesley fired again and drew his sword. He plunged toward the door, slashing his way with the sword, and one of the white men emptied a load of shot into his sword arm. Wesley crumpled to the ground, where he was immediately surrounded, kicked, and beaten. In the chaos, he saw that Craven had been shot in the face and was also being beaten, while Craven's younger brothers watched, too terrified to intervene.

The white men tied up Craven and dragged the

four fugitives off to the nearby town. Because of the seriousness of Wesley's wounds, he was taken to a local tavern and locked in a room on the second floor. There he was given medical care. After all, a dead slave was worthless, but a live one could bring money. Thirty-two shot pellets were removed from Wesley's arm, and his wounds were bandaged.

For two weeks, Wesley lay near death, suffering from fever, losing large amounts of blood. Although he was kept under strict watch, two sympathetic black people managed to communicate with him. One was the tavern cook. While bringing food to Wesley, she whispered the news that Craven and his brothers had been locked up in Westminster jail. At the end of three weeks, she brought worse news: the Mattersons had been taken down to Baltimore and sold for twelve hundred dollars apiece.

Wesley was shattered. The three brothers had come so close to freedom, and now the iron trap of slavery had closed over them again. Wesley made up his mind that he would not let that happen to him. He would make another effort to escape.

A second black person, named James Rogers, also found a way to get in touch with Wesley. He may have been the friendly black who had earlier warned the four fugitives that the area was dangerous. James Rogers agreed to help Wesley get away.

Wesley asked James to smuggle him a rope and three nails. One night, after he was left alone in the room, Wesley jammed the nails into the windowsill and tied the rope around them. Leaning out the window, he dropped his shoes to the ground. Then he sat on the windowsill, the rope between his teeth, and swung his legs over. The gaping wound in his arm wasn't fully healed, and he was still weak from loss of blood, but Wesley knew that his only chance for freedom lay outside the tavern.

Holding the rope with his good hand, using his bare feet to grip the rope, Wesley let himself down to the ground. The effort was exhausting, but he couldn't stop to rest. He hobbled through the darkness to a spot three-quarters of a mile away, where James was waiting to meet him.

The next morning, as news of the fugitive's escape spread through the surrounding area, James kept Wesley well hidden. Angry white men would soon be combing the countryside, so it was essential that Wesley leave as soon as possible. That night, provided with a strong horse and a guide to lead the way, Wesley set out on a back road for Gettysburg.

Wesley reached Gettysburg safely and found help from members of the Underground Railroad. He arrived in Philadelphia two weeks later, still suffering from his injuries but overjoyed to be in a city where a black person could breathe the air of freedom. William Still arranged medical treatment for Wesley's injuries and found a safe place for him to rest while he regained his strength. Most likely that safe location was in the Still home, with nursing care provided by William's wife, Letitia.

When Wesley was ready to travel, he was provided with clothes and a train ticket to Canada. It must have been a bittersweet moment when Wesley finally stepped onto Canadian soil. Now his freedom was guaranteed, but the Matterson brothers he had set out with were locked in slavery more firmly than ever.

≈ ≈ ≈

Wesley kept in touch with William Still after he reached Canada. When he became a naturalized citizen and found work on a railway line, Wesley wrote to tell William the good news. William must have smiled when he read that letter. The runaway slave who finished his trip to freedom with the help of the Underground Railroad was now earning his living as a brakeman on Canada's Great Western Railroad.

CHAPTER 10

JAMES MERCER, WILLIAM GILLIAM, AND JOHN CLAYTON

Covered with Coal Dust
February 1854

Steamboats carried passengers and freight from Southern cities like Richmond and Norfolk up the East Coast and into the Delaware River to Philadelphia. Free black people often worked as cooks and stewards on the steamers. Some risked harsh punishment by arranging secret passage for fugitive slaves they hid in a storeroom, behind the ship's boiler, or inside a cupboard meant for pots and pans. Once the steamer docked in Philadelphia, the non-paying passengers were smuggled off and guided to William Still. At any hour of the day or night, William and Letitia had to be prepared to welcome fugitives.

🔹 🔹 🔹

Down in Richmond, Virginia, the widow Louisa White had once owned thirty slaves. But Mrs. White ran into money problems. By February 1854, she had sold all but three of her slaves—James Mercer, William Gilliam, and a boy called Kit.

To add to her income, Mrs. White hired out James and William. Young and strong, both men were good workers. James, employed in a store, earned the widow $125 a year. William was a baker's assistant who also drove the bakery wagon. He brought the widow $135.

Recently, James had begun to worry about his future. He knew that money worries had led Mrs. White to take out a mortgage on him for $750. Sold at the slave market, James would easily bring $1200. The widow could sell James, pay off the mortgage, and still have money left over. William was also worried. If James was sold, William felt sure he would be next to go. The two men talked it over and decided to run away before Mrs. White had a chance to send them to the auction block.

James was married to a slave woman owned by a different master. James and his wife loved each other deeply, and he didn't want to leave her behind, but both knew the hard truth. For a strong young slave like James, the highest-paying market was in the deep South. If James was sold South, he and his wife would be separated forever, but if he managed to escape, perhaps she could follow him.

William and James had a friend named John Clayton, also a slave, who was employed in a tobacco factory. John Clayton learned that William and

James planned to run away and asked to go with them. All three had tried to escape previously, but those attempts had ended in failure. This time they were determined to succeed.

Because of their jobs, James, William, and John moved about the streets of Richmond. They came in contact with many people, white and black, and they had met a man who could help them. His name was Minkins.

Probably a free black, Minkins was employed on the steamship *Pennsylvania* traveling between Richmond and Philadelphia. But he also worked for the Underground Railroad. Just two months earlier, three fugitives had reached William Still, smuggled north by Minkins. Now Minkins agreed to arrange passage aboard the *Pennsylvania* for James, William, and John.

Late one night, when the steamship wharf was deserted, the men crept aboard the ship. Minkins led them to a cramped space near the boiler. Minkins told the men he wasn't sure they could survive the trip crowded into this small, uncomfortable hole, but it was the only hiding place available. James, William, and John didn't hesitate. The lure of freedom was too powerful. The three fugitives crawled into the tight space, determined to take the chance.

The journey lasted a day and a half, and during that time the men could barely move. The heat from the boiler was suffocating, and coal dust swirled in the air. Only one small opening provided ventilation. They took turns pressing up against the opening, struggling to catch a breath of fresh air.

At last, the steamer reached Philadelphia. It wasn't safe to leave the ship during daylight hours, so the fugitives remained huddled in their miserable hiding place far into the night. Finally, when the area around the waterfront had fallen quiet, a guide arrived to conduct them to William Still's house.

Icy rain drizzled down as the men stumbled through the dark streets. They reached William's house about three a.m. William must have seen a terrifying sight when he opened the door. The fugitives' faces and clothes, already streaked with soot, now dripped rain water as well. But James, William, and John were elated. They had reached Philadelphia. They had found freedom.

The words tumbled out as they told William Still about their difficult trip. William offered them a bath, and Letitia brought clean clothes. Imagine the pleasure those grimy travelers felt as they stripped off their filthy rags and stepped into a tub of hot water.

Slave catchers were an ever-present danger, so the men couldn't linger in Philadelphia. William arranged for them to travel north. By early March, the three fugitives had arrived in Canada.

Back in Richmond, their escape had caused an explosion of anger. William mailed the men an editorial he had clipped from *The Richmond Despatch*. The editorial writer announced indignantly that two slaves belonging to the Widow White had disappeared. He described James Mercer and William Gilliam as "uncommonly intelligent

Negroes"—as though their intelligence should have kept them from running away. William was a "tiptop baker" who had delivered bread to the steamer *Pennsylvania*, and the editorial writer was sure that seafaring characters William had met along the waterfront had helped him get off.

The writer believed that local white men— "Abolition scoundrels"—were also involved. Like many whites steeped in the culture of slavery, this Southern journalist couldn't believe that black people could manage a complicated, daring escape on their own.

From Canada, William Gilliam sent a letter back to Mrs. White in Richmond. Gleefully he informed her of his new estate in life. In her response, the angry widow accused William of acting dishonorably. "I am miserably poor, do not get a cent of your hire or James', besides losing you both," she complained. She mentioned young Kit, the remaining slave: "I fear, poor little fellow, that he will be obliged to go, as I am compelled to live, and it will be your fault. I am quite unwell, but of course, you don't care."

Mrs. White was right—William Gilliam didn't care. In a subsequent letter to William Still, he wrote that he had served Mrs. White as her slave for twenty-five years and two months. That was quite enough!

Almost a year after James' escape, his wife reached Philadelphia. Like James, she had traveled as a secret passenger on the steamship *Pennsylvania*. William Still arranged for her to continue on to

Toronto, Canada where her husband was waiting, his arms open to embrace her.

❧ ❧ ❧

Richmond authorities suspected that Minkins was involved in the escape of James, William, and John. Minkins was arrested and put in jail, but no evidence was found to convict him, and he was released. Imprisonment didn't cause him to regret his illegal behavior. Just eight months later another runaway arrived in Philadelphia by steamer, hidden on board by Minkins.

CHAPTER 11

CHARLES GILBERT

The Barking Dog and the Calico Dress
November 1854

The international slave trade officially ended in the United States in 1808. After that, no slaves could be imported. But in new states like Mississippi, Alabama, and Louisiana, plantations were expanding. Planters needed workers for their vast fields of cotton, sugar, and rice. Where would they find those workers?

The answer lay in states in the Upper South like Delaware, Maryland, and Virginia where owning slaves was becoming less profitable. Selling slaves into the Deep South quickly became a money-making business. Thousands were sold at auctions in cities like Washington and Richmond and shipped south for resale.

Slaves viewed that fate with horror. They had heard about cruel overseers and backbreaking labor performed in brutal heat under blazing sun. On cotton plantations, slaves worked ten hours a day in winter, fourteen hours a day in summer. During harvest time, they put in eighteen-hour days. Life was hard, escape almost impossible.

But even more than physical hardship, slaves feared the break-up of marriages and families. Over and over William Still heard fugitives speak of separations they had faced and losses they had endured. Husbands were torn from wives and children taken from parents, to be hurried off to the auction block.

To keep slaves in line, owners in the Upper South regularly threatened them with sale into the Deep South. Faced with that possibility, some slaves ran away. Charles Gilbert was one of them.

   ❜ ❜ ❜

Charles Gilbert was owned by a notorious Negro trader in Richmond, Virginia. The trader had been placing notices in Richmond newspapers offering to sell Charles the same way a farmer would advertise a goat or pig for sale. It was only a matter of time before someone bought him. Charles didn't want to be sold, and he didn't want to be owned. Not by the trader, not by anyone. He made up his mind to run away.

Charles had heard that the captain of a Boston schooner docked at Richmond might be willing to smuggle a fugitive slave north. He approached the captain, and the captain agreed to take him for a fee of ten dollars. Charles had the money, but there was another problem. The captain wanted to pick Charles up where the James River ran into the Chesapeake Bay at the tip of land called Old Point Comfort. That was 160 miles from Richmond.

Charles was familiar with Old Point Comfort. He had lived in that tiny town as a child and had friends and relatives in the area, including his mother, so he agreed to meet the schooner at that location. Somehow Charles managed to slip away from the trader and travel the long, dangerous miles to Old Point Comfort.

The slave trader was furious when he discovered that Charles had escaped. That slave was worth a lot of money! The trader advertised a reward of $200 for Charles' return and soon raised the amount to $550. The trader knew Charles had grown up in Old Point Comfort, so the ads mentioned that he might be found there. Eager for the reward, officers and slave catchers began combing the area for Charles.

With so many people hunting for him, Charles wasn't able to steal on board the schooner, and the captain left without him. It was a bitter blow, but Charles refused to give up. He wouldn't return to the slave trader no matter what.

He had to find a hiding place while he figured out what to do next. Charles' relatives couldn't help, not even his mother. They had been warned that they would face severe punishment if they assisted Charles in any way. A loyal friend hid Charles for a week, but the danger of discovery was too great. On his own, Charles found another hiding place, under a country hotel.

The Higee Hotel stood up on low pillars, and a water tank was located in the dusty space underneath the building. For four weeks Charles lived in that shallow crawl space, huddled in the shadows near the water cistern. His only food was scraps and peelings he took at night from the hotel slop tub.

One evening, a boy scrambled into the space under the hotel, hunting for some lost chickens. The youngster headed straight toward the water tank. Thinking quickly, Charles let out a savage bark followed by a low, threatening growl. Frightened, the boy scrambled out. His father, waiting for him, thought the dog was threatening his son. Charles heard the man say he'd hunt that dog down and kill him.

Terrified, Charles left the hotel that night and found his way into the center of a nearby woods. Even surrounded by thick bushes, he did not feel safe. Finally, he climbed an oak tree. For a full day Charles clung to a branch high up in the tree, weak with hunger and thirst, wondering what to do next. His situation was grim, his prospects bleak. But one thing Charles was sure of. He would not return to slavery.

Finally, Charles remembered a slave-woman he knew named Isabella. Isabella had charge of a wash-house where she laundered and ironed people's clothes. Under cover of darkness, Charles reached the wash-house and asked Isabella to hide him. Despite the risk, Isabella was willing, but she was concerned because the wash-house had no attic or secret closet where she could conceal a runaway slave. Charles told her about the dismal places where he had spent the past few weeks. He didn't need special comforts, he said. Perhaps a space could be made for him under the floor. Isabella agreed to help.

Only Isabella and one other friend named John Thomas knew about Charles' hiding place. During the day, stretched flat under the splintery floorboards, Charles could at least hear kind voices. At night when he came out, Isabella fed him and provided clean clothes. But after two weeks, Isabella heard alarming news—the wash-house was under suspicion.

Before Charles could get away, six officers arrived to search the wash-house. Isabella and John Thomas faced the officers, knowing full well that the fugitive the men were seeking was concealed under the floor they stood on. From his cramped hiding place, Charles heard the conversation. The officers offered $25 for help in finding Charles—a large sum of money for two poor slaves. But Isabella and John Thomas said they had no idea where Charles Gilbert was.

After the officers left, Charles knew he had to change locations. Like a hunted animal, he stole from place to place. He spent a week under the hotel . . . moved back to the woods . . . then into a swampy marsh. Finally, hungry and desperate, Charles returned to the dirt and spiders under the Higee Hotel.

Charles' mother had heard what was happening. She couldn't bear to see her son suffer that way. No matter how great the danger, she was determined to help him. With $40 of precious savings, Charles' mother arranged secret passage for her son on a steamer docked at Norfolk, just across the James River. That steamer would take Charles to Philadelphia.

Charles was relieved and happy. In one more day he would board the steamer and leave slavery behind. He decided to spend his last hours at the wash-house with Isabella, but he had been there only a short time when three officers strode across the yard.

Charles saw them approaching. By the time the officers entered, Charles had hurried upstairs and hidden inside a room hung with women's clothing. While two of the officers questioned Isabella about boarders who sometimes stayed in her house, the third man said he'd look upstairs.

As the officer started toward the wooden stairway, Charles heard his footsteps. Only a thin curtain concealed Charles from the approaching officer. In a flash, Charles grabbed an old calico dress and yanked it over his head. He pulled on a bonnet, tugged the brim low on his forehead, and pushed through the curtain.

As Charles started down the stairs, the surprised officer looked up at him. "Whose gal are you?" he asked.

"Mr. Cockling's, sir," Charles drawled in a soft voice.

"What is your name?"

"Delie, sir."

"Go on then!" said the officer impatiently. Charles went all right—out the door and away to the steamer.

Another nail-biting delay lay ahead. The steamer remained in Norfolk for four weeks. During that time, Charles had to stay hidden, always fearful of discovery. Finally the ship started north.

On November 11, the steamer docked in Philadelphia. Soon Charles was telling his remarkable story to William Still. Charles Gilbert had been on the run for months. At last, thanks to his own quick wits and determination and the help of others, he had found the road to freedom.

ہے ہے ہے

The Philadelphia Anti-Slavery Society received several Southern newspapers, including *The Baltimore Sun, The Richmond Dispatch,* and *The Richmond Enquirer.* Reading the Southern newspapers, William Still paid special attention to columns headed by a drawing of a black man with a bundle on his back. These columns contained ads for runaway slaves like the notices the slave trader had placed in his efforts to recapture Charles Gilbert.

The ads named the fugitives, told the location they had escaped from, and offered a reward for their return. Often the ad included the fugitive's age, shade of skin color, and general body build. Distinctive details were mentioned: a mark on the fugitive's neck . . . a scar above the eye . . . a broken tooth. Some descriptions were so accurate that William recognized runaway slaves who came to him in Philadelphia before they told him their names or said where they were from.

The newspapers carried these ads to benefit Southern slaveholders, but William Still used them in very different ways. Upon reading that a slave had recently escaped, he directed members of the Vigilance Committee to watch for that individual on the streets of Philadelphia. In addition, William sent copies of ads to "stockholders," people whose donations helped finance the Underground Railroad. These ads provided a disturbing look into a system that hunted human beings like animals.

CHAPTER 12

JANE JOHNSON

Come Down to Bloodgood's Hotel
July 1855

* * *

Slaves brought into a free state by their owners were entitled to freedom. State laws were clear on that point, but Southern slave owners sometimes brought slaves along anyway. Perhaps they had convinced themselves that their slaves had no desire to be free. Perhaps they didn't believe that the law would be enforced. Or perhaps, as William Still observed, they simply felt it didn't apply to them.

* * *

At 4:30 on a warm summer afternoon, a black boy burst into the anti-slavery office and handed a folded scrap of paper to William Still. Inside, William found a hastily scribbled message:

> Mr. Still—Sir: Will you come down to Bloodgood's Hotel as soon as possible—as

there are three fugitive slaves here and they
want liberty. Their master is here with them,
on his way to New York.

If a slave wanted freedom, the Vigilance
Committee was ready to help. William ran to the
nearby office of Passmore Williamson, the committee's only white member.

William knew that the presence of both a black
and a white man would be essential in this delicate
situation. A slave hoping to claim freedom would
have to act in the face of an angry master. The
presence of William, a black man, would encourage
the slave's confidence while Passmore Williamson,
with his light skin, would represent the kind of
authority a white Southerner was accustomed to
dealing with. That would make it more difficult for
the slave owner to intimidate his servant.

Passmore Williamson had been about to leave
for the state capital on business but decided to delay
his journey. He and William had to act immediately. The two men hurried to Bloodgood's Hotel,
located by the ferry wharf.

William stepped inside and scanned the hotel
lobby. He saw a few black employees, including the
boy who had brought him the note, but no sign of
the slaves they were seeking. Now what?

An employee edged closer. Quietly he told
William that the people he was looking for had just
boarded the ferry to New Jersey. William asked
what they looked like. "A tall, dark woman with
two little boys," came the reply.

William rejoined Passmore Williamson, and they hurried across the wharf and onto the ferry. It was almost departure time, and William saw no passengers who resembled the three slaves they were looking for. But word of what was happening had been sent ahead to black ferry workers. One of them nodded toward the stairway and said: "They are up on the second deck."

Quickly William and Passmore Williamson mounted the stairs. On the upper level sat a somber-looking black woman accompanied by two boys. Seated nearby was a white man holding a cane.

William and Passmore Williamson didn't know that the white man was Colonel John Wheeler, recently appointed U.S. Minister to Nicaragua. Wheeler had traveled up to Philadelphia from Washington and was now headed for New York where he would board a ship for Nicaragua. Wheeler's wife was waiting for him in Nicaragua, and Wheeler was taking along, as a servant for his wife, a young slave woman named Jane Johnson and Jane's two sons.

William and Passmore Williamson faced a complicated situation. They had to make sure that this black woman really was a slave who had been brought into Pennsylvania by her owner and that she did, indeed, want freedom. With those facts established, they could explain her legal rights and offer assistance. They would have to manage all this in the presence of the owner, who would certainly object.

William spoke first. "Are you traveling?" he asked.

"Yes," Jane Johnson replied.

"With whom?"

She nodded to the man beside her.

"Do they belong to you, Sir?" William asked.

Frowning at the question, Colonel Wheeler responded curtly, "Yes, they are in my charge."

Now Passmore Williamson and William both addressed Jane. Rapidly they told her that she was entitled to freedom under the laws of Pennsylvania. Judges in the city of Philadelphia had decided many cases like hers in favor of freedom. If she wanted to remain a slave, they could not force her to leave, but they wanted to be sure she was aware of her rights.

Colonel Wheeler interrupted angrily. The woman knew all about the laws, he said. She didn't want to leave him. She was traveling to New York to see friends.

It was a tense moment. Jane Johnson had to trust two men she didn't know—had never even seen before. But Jane did not hesitate. In a firm voice, she said that she wanted her freedom. She had always wanted to be free.

The bell was sounding, a signal that the ferry was about to depart. William touched Jane's arm lightly. "Come with us," he urged quietly. Jane rose, taking her sons by the hand, and went with William Still toward the stairway.

Colonel Wheeler sprang to his feet, pushing his way after Jane and protesting to Passmore Williamson. As they reached the lower deck, Wheeler tried to grab Jane, and her younger son burst into tears. Suddenly, five black porters appeared around them, clearly sympathetic to the mother and her children.

Shielded by the porters, William kept Jane and the boys moving, off the ferry and onto the wharf, while Colonel Wheeler argued with Passmore Williamson. William beckoned to a carriage, helped Jane and the boys inside, and leaped up beside them. The carriage rolled off leaving Wheeler behind, still objecting furiously.

Several blocks away, William paid the driver and sent him off. Then he hurried Jane and the boys to a temporary hiding place and returned to the office. Checking the time, William was pleased to see that the whole escape had taken place in less than an hour.

That night, under cover of darkness, William smuggled Jane and the children to his own home. He and Letitia listened attentively as Jane told them about the events that had brought her to Philadelphia.

Colonel Wheeler was a wealthy man who had once owned between thirty and forty slaves. Over the past two years, he had sold those slaves, perhaps expecting his recent government appointment. During the same period, he had bought Jane and two of her sons from a Richmond slave owner. A third boy had been left behind in Richmond, and Jane had no hope that she would ever see him again.

Earlier in the day, Wheeler, Jane, and the two boys had traveled from Washington to Philadelphia by train. They had stopped off in the city to visit

Colonel Wheeler's father-in-law. Jane had heard the father-in-law warn Wheeler that he could not have done a worse thing than to bring slaves into Pennsylvania. Wheeler had stated confidently that Jane would not leave him, words he would come to regret. Jane had made up her mind to seek freedom the first chance she got.

Delayed by their visit to the father-in-law, Wheeler and his slaves arrived late at the wharf and missed the two o'clock ferry. Now they would have to wait till five to depart. Colonel Wheeler took Jane and the boys into nearby Bloodgood's Hotel. Despite his outward show of confidence, the colonel was keeping a close eye on his slaves. He found a quiet place where they could wait and warned Jane not to talk with the black help. Then he went into the dining room for dinner.

In the midst of his meal, Wheeler came out to check on Jane. She was standing calmly by a banister close to the spot where he had left her. Reassured, the colonel returned to the dining room.

Actually Jane had been watching for someone who might help her. Twice, she managed to speak with a black employee. Each time, she explained that she and her sons were slaves who wanted freedom and needed help. The employees were sympathetic but couldn't promise anything. However, one of them sent an urgent note to William Still. Jane had no idea that help might be on the way, and as they left the hotel and boarded the ferry, her hopes faded.

Knowing that Colonel Wheeler was a Democrat

with high connections, William felt sure he would turn to the federal court to try to recover his slaves. Jane and the boys had to be removed from Wheeler's reach. William immediately made arrangements for them to travel to abolitionists in New York City who would keep them safely hidden.

William Still was right about Wheeler. That very evening, Wheeler obtained a writ of habeas corpus signed by Judge John Kintzing Kane that ordered Passmore Williamson to produce the slaves. Wheeler's decision to name Passmore Williamson in the writ rather than William Still seemed curious since William was the person who actually drove off with the slaves. But Wheeler, with the mind-set of a typical Southern slave-owner, obviously believed that the white man must be the person responsible for the event.

The writ was delivered that night to Passmore Williamson's father, who brought it to William Still the following morning. The elderly Quaker told William that his son had already left on his business trip and added, "Thee had better attend to it."

William met with members of the Vigilance Committee to plot their strategy. A lawyer was sent to Independence Hall to explain to Judge Kane why Passmore Williamson hadn't come to answer the writ. Judge Kane had earlier presided over the hearing for Euphemia Williams and the Christiana riot trial. Although those matters had turned out well, William Still knew that Kane was generally unsympathetic toward abolitionists and would take a stern position on this matter.

The next day, back from his trip, Passmore Williamson came to see William Still. He asked just one question: Were Jane and the children safe? William assured him that they were. Not a word was spoken about where William had first taken the slaves or where they were now located.

When Passmore Williamson responded to the writ of habeas corpus, he stated truthfully that the three slaves had never been in his custody, and he didn't know where they were. Judge Kane knew he was being outwitted. Furious, he charged Williamson with contempt of court and had him locked up in Moyamensing Prison. William Still was also arrested as were the five black dock workers on charges ranging from forcible abduction and riot to assault and battery.

As news of the incident flew through the city, strong feelings sprang up on both sides. Pro-slavery sympathizers argued that abolitionists and Negroes had no right to interfere with a Southern gentleman passing through Philadelphia with his slaves. Opponents of slavery insisted that the laws of the free state of Pennsylvania had to be respected, even by Southern gentlemen.

The six black men were to be tried first. Colonel Wheeler had been claiming publicly that Jane had not left him of her own free will—she had been abducted. The anti-slavery forces realized that it was essential for Jane to testify in person. James McKim arranged to have Jane travel down secretly from New York for the trial.

Accompanied by several abolitionist women

from the Philadelphia area, Jane entered the court-room with a veil hiding her face. When testimony began, the name "Jane Johnson" was called. Murmurs of shock and surprise ran through the courtroom as Jane lifted her veil and walked to the witness stand. Calmly, Jane testified that she had always desired her freedom. When she was offered the opportunity to leave her owner, she took that opportunity willingly.

Jane's strong testimony and dignified manner undercut the prosecution's case. Thanks to her testimony, William Still, tried first, was acquitted of all charges. The five dock workers, tried next, were found not guilty on the charge of riot. However, during the argument on the wharf, two of the black workers had come in physical contact with Colonel Wheeler. That was enough for the court to find them guilty of assault and battery. Their punishment: one week in jail.

The outcome of the trial satisfied Jane's supporters, but the threat of danger still hung over the courtroom. The U.S. Marshall was present, holding a warrant for Jane's arrest, along with the U.S. District Attorney, who had sworn to take her into custody. Officers of the State of Pennsylvania were also in the courtroom determined to resist the federal officers and let Jane leave freely, protected by state laws. Rumors had said that a conflict might break out at the door.

The situation was tense, but the police officers surrounding Jane caught federal officials by surprise when they rushed her unexpectedly out a rear entrance to the courtroom. Jane emerged safely from Independence Hall and rode off in a carriage accompanied by James McKim, abolitionist Lucretia Mott, and a city police officer. A second carriage followed, bearing more police officers for additional protection.

Jane's right to freedom had been assured, but Passmore Williamson remained in prison. Judge Kane insisted that Williamson had given a false response to the writ of habeas corpus and must change his statement. Passmore Williamson insisted that he had spoken the truth and had no reason to change his response in any way. Neither man would give in, and Williamson's prison stay stretched into weeks and then months.

Judge Kane, outraged at being defied, intended the confinement as punishment. Instead, the prison sentence turned into a great success for the anti-slavery cause. Publicity concerning the Jane Johnson case spread, and anger over Passmore Williamson's confinement kept increasing. Many prominent people came to visit him in prison, and letters expressing sympathy arrived from all over the North. The judge was caught in a contest of wills he couldn't win. Three months after he sent Passmore Williamson to jail, Judge Kane released him.

ða ða ða

Following the trial, Jane Johnson returned to New York City. Later she moved to Boston with her sons. She found work, and her boys attended school. One of her sons later went to sea. The second son served in the Civil War with the 55th Massachusetts Regiment of U.S. Black Troops. There is no record of what happened to Jane's third son, separated from her in Virginia so many years earlier.

CHAPTER 13

WILLIAM STILL IN CANADA

Shaking Hands with the Lion's Paw
September 1855

Fugitives arriving in Philadelphia often told William Still that they intended to shake hands with the lion's paw. That meant they hoped to travel up to Canada. Canada was part of the British Empire, and the lion was a symbol of that empire. Since the British had outlawed slavery in 1833, any slave who entered Canada was automatically free.

Slave owners were well aware of this fact and painted a grim picture of Canada for their slaves. They described deep snows, terrible suffering, and starvation. They hinted that cruel Canadians often carried fugitives off to another country and sold them back into slavery. However, stories like this often had the opposite effect from the one the slave owner intended. If the slave owner said Canada was a terrible place for black people, the slave felt sure it was exactly the place he ought to head for.

William Still received many letters from fugitives who had escaped to Canada, but he wanted to see for himself what kind of life they found there. In September 1855, William made a trip north. Visiting a number of Canadian settlements where runaway slaves were living, William found fugitives in good spirits and well able to care for themselves.

One town he visited was Chatham. Some time after he returned, a Philadelphia newspaper reported that conflicts between white and black people had broken out in Chatham, and riots were possible. "The hate of races has begun in Canada," the newspaper warned.

William knew better. He wrote a response to the article that said most blacks in Chatham were industrious, peaceable, and prosperous. Black people had built churches, schools, and fire companies. They worked at many trades, including masonry, plastering, and carpentry. They made shoes and repaired watches. In the Chatham market, black farmers sold produce they had grown on their own land.

William acknowledged that there were probably some black people in Chatham who were poor, lazy, or inclined to crime and drunkenness. "But," he asked pointedly, "couldn't the same be said of white people, even those who had grown up with every advantage?"

ANN MARIA WEEMS

Alias Joe
November 1855

During the 1840s, Washington, D.C., had been an important center of the domestic slave trade. Visitors from abroad were horrified to see lines of slaves bound by chains trudging through the streets of the capital. Slave pens and auction blocks were scattered throughout the city, with one auction even held directly across from the White House in Lafayette Square.

As part of the Compromise of 1850, slave auctions were abolished in Washington, but slavery remained legal for twelve years after that. During that period, a courageous young slave girl escaped from the city assisted by a Washington lawyer and a Philadelphia physician identified as "Dr. H." Without help from William Still, that flight to freedom could not have taken place.

❧ ❧ ❧

On a chilly November day, a horse and carriage waited in front of the White House near grassy Lafayette Square. A dark-skinned young coachman sat erect on the carriage seat while, beside the buggy, the owner concluded a conversation with another gentleman. The two white men shook hands, and the owner stepped into the carriage. "Drive on, Joe," he ordered. The coachman flicked the reins, and the horse trotted off.

The buggy owner was a prominent physician from Philadelphia. Anyone seeing the satisfied expression on his face might have thought that the White House had just informed him that he was going to receive some honor. That guess would have been wrong. In fact, Dr. H. was breaking the law. His black "coachman" was a fifteen-year-old girl dressed in boy's clothing—a runaway slave. The doctor and Ann Maria Weems were starting a dangerous journey together.

Ann Maria had been the property of a slave trader in Rockville, Maryland—a rough man who drank and used foul language. His wife was equally ill-tempered. Ann Maria had seen her mistreat a young slave boy. Ann Maria believed the woman disliked the child because her husband—Ann Maria's owner—was the boy's father. No wonder Ann Maria wanted to escape!

Friends who were willing to help tried to buy Ann Maria. A Washington lawyer named J. Bigelow made an offer on their behalf, but Ann Maria's owner refused to sell this smart, good-looking girl.

Mr. Bigelow had heard about the work William

Still was doing with the Vigilance Committee in Philadelphia. He wrote to William asking for his help. Mr. Bigelow offered $300 in expense money to any agent of the Underground Railroad who would take Ann Maria to New York.

He explained that Ann Maria was enslaved about ten or twelve miles outside Washington. To prepare for the trip north, Ann Maria would first be smuggled into the city. She would be kept in hiding until public outcry over her disappearance had died down. Then it would be safe for the agent and Ann Maria to start north.

William was sympathetic, but the Vigilance Committee assisted fugitives only after they reached Philadelphia. The committee didn't send agents South to encourage slaves to run away or to help them leave their owners. Nevertheless, William promised Mr. Bigelow that he would personally try to find someone who could assist Ann Maria.

William began searching for a person brave and skillful enough to take on the task. He spoke with two sea captains who sometimes smuggled slaves to freedom, but both had trips scheduled to other locations.

Time was passing. Mr. Bigelow wrote to say that plans at his end were moving forward. He had received word that the merchandise would soon be delivered. In the secret code of the Underground Railroad, "merchandise" meant runaway slaves. Ann Maria was about to be brought to Washington, and William hadn't yet found a way for her to travel north.

A few weeks later Mr. Bigelow sent another letter. He described ads that had appeared in *The Baltimore Sun* offering rewards for four runaway slaves. One of those slaves was Ann Maria. William knew Mr. Bigelow was telling him that Ann Maria had reached Washington and was now under his protection. But the difficult question remained— how could this dangerous merchandise be safely shipped north?

William struggled to come up with a solution. Finally, he turned to his family physician. Dr. H. was "a true friend of the slave," a person who supported the Underground Railroad though he wasn't actively involved. William asked if Dr. H. would travel to Washington and bring Ann Maria back.

Dr. H. understood the risks. If he was caught, he would face fines, public prosecution, perhaps even prison. Nevertheless, he agreed to take on the dangerous task. But he couldn't leave right away. Dr. H. was on the staff of a Philadelphia medical college, and classes were in session. He couldn't make the trip until Thanksgiving break, six weeks away. Mr. Bigelow would have to keep Ann Maria hidden until then. The long delay would be dangerous, but William could think of no other solution.

While they waited, details of the trip were worked out. It was decided that Ann Maria would travel as the doctor's coachman and answer to the name Joe Wright. To conceal the fact that she was a girl, she would wear a deep cap, a black coat over a shirt and vest, pantaloons, and a bow tie. While she waited down in Washington, Ann Maria put on her coachman's clothes every day and practiced moving and speaking like a boy.

At last Dr. H. arrived. For safety's sake, Mr. Bigelow had asked the doctor to meet him and Ann Maria near the White House, rather than at the lawyer's own residence a few blocks away. Now, with the conversation ended and Ann Maria in the coachman's seat, the dangerous trip north was underway.

As the buggy rolled through the streets of Washington, Dr. H. worried about a serious problem. Traveling north through Maryland, he planned to take back roads so that they would meet as few people as possible. But that longer route also meant they would have to spend one night at a tavern or farmhouse before reaching the Pennsylvania border. A $500 reward was offered for Ann Maria, so every encounter would hold the threat of danger.

As a young man, Dr. H. had sometimes visited the area he intended to travel through, and he had formed a friendship with a local farmer. At the end of the day's journey, the doctor and Ann Maria would pass near the farmer's property. Dr. H. decided to make the farmhouse their destination.

He warned Ann Maria that the overnight stay presented serious risks. The farmer was a slave owner. Ann Maria would have to play her coachman role in front of the farmer's family and his slaves as well. No one must suspect that she was not what she appeared to be.

Ann Maria knew the consequences to the doctor and to herself if she was found out. She would certainly be whipped. Worse, she might be sold South into conditions far more brutal than she lived under in Maryland. That prospect was very real to Ann Maria. Earlier, three of her brothers had been taken from her parents and sold South.

As night fell, the buggy rolled to a stop at the farmhouse door. The farmer and his wife were delighted to welcome their old acquaintance. Dr. H. explained that he was returning to Philadelphia along this back-country route because he hadn't been feeling well. He believed the sight of familiar places and people would do him good.

The farmer and his wife spared no pains to make their distinguished guest comfortable. Soon they were sitting in the parlor chatting about farming, the doctor's medical practice, and matters pertaining to slavery. Imagine their shock if they had known that their guest was traveling with a runaway slave. Meanwhile, out in the kitchen, Ann Maria worked hard to maintain her disguise in front of the family slaves.

After dinner, the doctor said he wasn't feeling well and would retire early. He wanted his coachman to sleep in the same room with him in case he needed help during the night. "Simply give him a bed quilt," said the doctor, "and he will fare well enough in one corner of the room." The doctor and the coachman slept soundly, the doctor in the bed and "Joe" wrapped in a quilt on the floor.

The next morning Doctor H. and his coachman continued their journey. At some point they crossed the Mason-Dixon Line into Pennsylvania. But Ann Maria wasn't safe yet. If discovered, she could easily be taken back to her owner. The doctor instructed Ann Maria not to reveal her true identity or tell anyone where she had come from until she was alone with William Still.

At four in the afternoon, the carriage drew up in front of the Still house. William was out, but Mrs. Still was at home with another fugitive and the family's hired girl. Dr. H. couldn't wait till William returned—he was eager to let his worried wife know he had returned safely. He simply told Mrs. Still that he wanted to leave the boy with her and hurried off.

Letitia Still was accustomed to strangers showing up at her home. She told the young coachman to wait in the dining room, and "Joe" obediently took a chair.

When William returned, he was elated to learn that Dr. B. had brought a boy to the house. William went into the dining room, confident that this was the merchandise he had been expecting from Washington. Instead, the young coachman told William that he had come from York, Pennsylvania. Puzzled, William asked why the doctor had brought him to the Stills' house. Instead of replying, the boy walked outside, and William followed. When Ann Maria was alone with William, she revealed her identity. Other people were present in the house, she explained, so she had earlier told William exactly what the doctor had instructed her to say.

William was impressed by Ann Maria's poise

and courage. When he explained the situation to his wife, she was astonished to discover that the well-dressed "boy" who had waited in her dining room was actually a girl. Ann Maria had played her part perfectly.

Ann Maria stayed hidden in Philadelphia for a few days. Then William sent her on to New York disguised in her coachman's coat, pantaloons, and cap. Ann Maria was taken to the house of Lewis Tappan, a well-to-do merchant and confirmed abolitionist. It was Thanksgiving weekend, and Tappan's house was filled with guests. Ann Maria was placed in a comfortable upstairs room with the door locked so that no one could walk in unexpectedly. Safe from discovery, Ann Maria enjoyed her own Thanksgiving feast of turkey and plum pudding.

Ann Maria had relatives living in the Canadian community of Dresden, a haven for runaway slaves. Lewis Tappan arranged with the pastor of a black church in nearby Brooklyn to accompany Ann Maria north by train to find her relatives. A wardrobe of girl's clothes was provided for her to take along, but for safety sake Ann Maria traveled in her boy's disguise.

Reverend Freeman, the pastor escorting Ann Maria, knew of the large reward offered for her return. As the train moved north through New York State, he feared trouble at every stop. His anxiety grew as the train approached the bridge at Niagara Falls. Fugitives often used that bridge to cross into Canada, and slave-catchers often waited there to pounce on them. To Reverend Freeman's relief, the train passed over the bridge and emerged onto Canadian soil without incident. Ann Maria was finally free.

That night Reverend Freeman and Ann Maria stopped in Chatham, the town William Still had visited just two months earlier. More than three thousand fugitives had settled in that town. Reverend Freeman and Ann Maria planned to spend the night at a local boarding house.

When they arrived, a group of boarders and neighbors were chatting in the sitting room. Reverend Freeman asked to speak privately with the landlord. He explained that the boy accompanying him was actually a young girl fleeing slavery. The girl had traveled all the way from Washington, D.C. in disguise. "She would be very glad now to be able to change her clothes," he said.

The astonished landlord called his wife, who quickly summoned the other women in the house. The women disappeared upstairs with Joe—and returned with Ann Maria. In a letter Reverend Freeman sent back to Lewis Tappan, he described what happened when the women introduced Miss Ann Maria Weems to the group gathered in the sitting room: "The whole company were on their feet, shook hands, laughed, and rejoiced, declaring that this beat all they had ever seen before."

Two days later, Reverend Freeman and Ann Maria approached their final destination—the village of Dresden. As they walked toward the village, they met Ann Maria's uncle on the road. The astonished man exclaimed, "My Lord! Maria, is that you?" He took them to his house where his wife greeted her niece with tears of joy. "Such a scene I had never before witnessed," wrote Reverend Freeman. "She, who had been given up as lost, was now found!"

Ann Maria's uncle and aunt had escaped from slavery just four years earlier. Now they owned two farms and were worth three thousand dollars. Southern owners claimed that slaves were incapable of caring for themselves. Fugitives like Ann Maria's uncle and aunt proved that wasn't so.

William Still was glad to learn that Ann Maria had found a loving home in a place where she could receive an education and find a future. Reverend Freeman returned to Brooklyn rejoicing that he had been to a land where black people were free.

ʚ ʚ ʚ

Dresden, the Canadian town where Ann Maria's aunt and uncle prospered, had a long history of welcoming fugitives. Some years earlier, a slave from Kentucky named Josiah Henson had settled there with his wife and four children. Henson started the first North American vocational school for black people, a place where fugitives could learn farming and other practical skills needed to earn a living. Josiah Henson realized that people like Ann Maria and her relatives would only be truly free when they were able to support themselves.

HARRIET EGLIN AND
CHARLOTTE GILES

Dressed in Black
May 1856

Often, runaway slaves escaped by making themselves invisible. They traveled by night, in darkness. They hid inside caves and hollow trees. They crawled into shipping crates or crouched beneath the deck of a schooner.

A few fugitives, however, made the dangerous journey right under the eyes of white authorities. They traveled unnoticed, by putting on disguises that kept them from detection. Ellen Craft had dressed as a Southern gentleman. Ann Maria Weems had passed herself off as a coachman. In the following story, two other young women created their own clever masquerade to fool hostile whites.

୬ ୬ ୬

Harriet Eglin and Charlotte Giles were cousins, owned by two different masters in the city of

Baltimore. Like most slaves, these young women couldn't read or write. Nevertheless, they found the courage to run away and the imagination to succeed.

They made their way north in broad daylight, riding the train from Baltimore to Philadelphia. To conceal their identity they depended on a simple strategy—they wore dark mourning clothes, as though they were traveling to a funeral.

When Harriet and Charlotte came up with the idea, they knew that they couldn't bring along any luggage. The sight of two young black women carrying carpet bags was sure to raise suspicion that they were running away. Harriet and Charlotte decided that they would leave extra clothing with their uncle in Baltimore. When they were settled in a safe location, he could send them a package containing the clothes.

Their plan was simple but daring. Imagine two women seated on a train, faces covered by thick black veils, heads bent in sorrow. They would wear black dresses, and each would carry a crumpled handkerchief in her gloved hand. Surely no one would disturb these grief-stricken women, obviously traveling to a funeral.

But before they could put their plan in motion, Harriet and Charlotte had to find a way to board that train. They faced the same problem William and Ellen Craft had encountered earlier. The train from Baltimore to Philadelphia offered direct transportation from a slave state to a free state, so railway authorities in Baltimore were always on the watch for runaways. To purchase tickets, Harriet and Charlotte needed a reputable person, someone familiar to the agent, who would vouch that they were free to travel to Philadelphia.

Fortunately, Harriet and Charlotte knew such a person—a friend named James Adams who was a black man well-known in Baltimore. Adams agreed to help. On May 31, James Adams escorted Harriet and Charlotte to the station. They purchased their tickets, said good-bye to James, and boarded the train.

It was late spring, when the weather turns warm in Baltimore. Weighed down by their heavy dresses, barely able to breathe behind their thick veils, the women waited nervously for the train to depart.

Suddenly a man they recognized rushed into the car. It was the dry-goods merchant who owned one of the women. He approached the terrified young women and peered through their heavy veils. "What is your name?" he demanded of Charlotte. "Mary, sir," she sobbed. He repeated the question to Harriet. In a faint voice Harriet replied, "Lizzie, sir." Impatiently the merchant turned away and hurried on to another car. Charlotte and Harriet held their breath. Finally, through the train window, they saw him leave the station.

How could the slave owner fail to recognize his own property? Perhaps the black veils blurred the young women's features. Or perhaps a white Southern male simply couldn't believe that inexperienced slaves, young women who could neither read nor write, would be bold enough to attempt such a daring disguise.

A few hours later, Harriet and Charlotte arrived in Philadelphia. The Vigilance Committee was expecting them, and an escort guided them from the train station to William Still's house. There, Harriet and Charlotte threw back the thick veils to reveal their smiling faces. William and Letitia were no doubt amused when they learned how cleverly the young women had carried off the deception.

William knew that news of their escape would reach Philadelphia quickly. Slave hunters might already be watching for them on the streets and at railway stations, so he decided to keep the young women in hiding for a few days. Letitia treated them with the kindness she showed all fugitives who found refuge at the Stills' home. During the time they stayed in Philadelphia, Charlotte asked someone from the Still household to write to their uncle in Baltimore concerning the clothes he was keeping for her and Harriet. That letter proved to be a serious mistake.

By 1856, the Underground Railroad was well established in New York State, and William had contacts with stationmasters in several different locations. He arranged for Harriet and Charlotte to travel to the city of Syracuse where an Underground Railroad agent named Jermain Wesley Loguen took charge of the young women. Thanks to Loguen's contacts, two anti-slavery families from a nearby village offered to take the young women in and give them work. Harriet and Charlotte accepted.

Harriet asked someone to write to William for

her. The message described the cousins' experiences since leaving Philadelphia. Harriet also mentioned the letter Charlotte had earlier sent to their uncle. Charlotte had asked the uncle to send a parcel of clothes to William, and Harriet asked if William would kindly forward that package to Mr. Loguen.

William wrote back with disturbing news. Charlotte's letter to their uncle had been intercepted and read by the slave owner. The slave owner had found clues in the letter that helped him figure out how the two women got out of Baltimore. As a result, James Adams had been arrested and was now in prison, charged with helping fugitive slaves escape.

Harriet was greatly upset by what had happened. She sent William another letter, telling him that Charlotte had become unhappy with her situation after just one week and moved on to Canada. Harriet was angry with her cousin. She hoped Charlotte hadn't sent other letters to Baltimore that might reveal Harriet's location or cause trouble for people who had been kind to them.

William soon heard further news regarding James Adams. His situation looked grim. Helping slaves escape was a serious offense, and James was a black man facing trial before a white court. But the angry slave owner made a mistake. In addition to charging Adams with the loss of his slave, he also sued the railroad. Unlike James Adams, the railway company had money and power with which to contest the suit.

At the trial, attorneys for the railway company

established the fact that the owner had come to the station hunting for his runaway slave. He had entered a railway car, spoken to two young women, and left convinced that neither was his slave. In fact, he had said as much to the train conductor. Therefore, the attorneys argued, there was no evidence that the railway company had failed to do its duty. In fact, there wasn't even any proof that the women on the train were the runaway slaves.

Thanks to the skill of the railway attorneys, the jury returned a verdict of not guilty for both parties. James Adams was released, and the railway company paid the slave owner nothing. In addition to losing his valuable slave, the owner was obliged to pay the costs of taking the suit to court. For all who despised slavery, it was a satisfying outcome.

Several months later, Harriet wrote again to William. She assured him that she was happy in New York State and wished that her brothers and sisters in slavery were as well off as she was. One more thing—Harriet told William that she was learning to read and write.

‌ ‌ ‌

The Underground Railroad agent who helped Harriet and Charlotte in Syracuse was Jermain Wesley Loguen, a school teacher, minister, and fugitive from slavery.

Friends in Syracuse had offered to purchase Loguen's freedom so that he wouldn't need to worry about being recaptured, but Loguen turned them down, declaring that he had already received his freedom from Heaven. When the Fugitive Slave Act of 1850 caused many fugitives to flee to Canada, Loguen wouldn't go. He said he did not fear that law and had no intention of obeying it.

In 1851, Loguen and other abolitionists rescued a fugitive whose owner had pursued him from Missouri all the way up to Syracuse. The incident caused a sensation, and authorities resolved to arrest Loguen and the other abolitionists involved. Loguen had no choice at that point—he had to seek temporary refuge in Canada. But as soon as it was safe to return, the Reverend Jermain Wesley Loguen came back to Syracuse and continued his work with the Underground Railroad.

CHAPTER 16

SIX RUNAWAYS FROM MARYLAND

Four Large and Two Small Hams
May 1856

❧ ❧ ❧

By the middle of the 19th century, telegraph
lines connected many American cities. This
new form of rapid communication helped slave
owners who sometimes sent telegraph messages
to arrange the capture of runaways. But workers
on the Underground Railroad also used the
telegraph—to help fugitives escape. At times,
they included code words in their messages to
conceal the meaning from outsiders.

❧ ❧ ❧

The day Harriet and Charlotte arrived at
William Still's house, two other groups of runaways
had already arrived. William and Letitia had eight
people to care for, eight people to keep hidden
from slave catchers. William went back to the office
after dinner with much on his mind. He found
a member of the mayor's police force waiting to

113

speak with him.

The officer told William that he had received a telegram from a slaveholder in Hagerstown, Maryland. Six slaves had run away from that area, and the slaveholder knew that they had reached Harrisburg, Pennsylvania. He believed that they were now on board a train leaving Harrisburg and headed to Philadelphia. His telegram promised the officer a reward of $1,300 to meet the train and arrest the slaves.

But the officer wasn't interested in earning the reward. "I would have nothing to do with the contemptible work of arresting fugitives," he told William firmly. "I'd rather help them off." The officer planned to notify the slave owner that he would watch for the fugitives. Instead, he wanted William to send a member of the Vigilance Committee to the train depot to convey the fugitives to safety.

The officer was a stranger to William. Could he be trusted? William decided that he could. As they were talking, William had noticed a telegram lying on his desk, delivered while he was at dinner. William suspected that the telegram contained information about the runaway slaves. Explaining that to the officer, William tore open the telegram. Inside he found this curious message:

Harrisburg, May 31st, 1856

Wm. Still, N. 5th St.:—I have sent via at two o'clock four large and two small hams.

Jos. C. Bustill

William told the officer that the telegram did contain information about the runaways, but he didn't show him the message. The man wouldn't have understood it anyway.

Joseph Bustill, the person who sent the telegram, was an Underground Railroad conductor in Harrisburg who had forwarded fugitives to William in the past. Bustill often used code words in his telegrams to William in case the message was intercepted. "Hams" were runaway slaves. "Four large" meant four adults and "two small" were children.

Bustill had put the six "hams" on a train to Philadelphia, but they weren't headed for the Harrisburg depot at Eleventh and Market Streets where the policeman expected them. The code word "via" had given William a secret message. Bustill was sending those "hams" on the Reading line, which ended at a different station. The officer could have waited all night at Eleventh and Market Streets without catching sight of the fugitives.

William thanked the officer and assured him that he would handle the matter. After he left, William sent someone from the Vigilance Committee to meet the Reading train, and the "hams" came safely into his custody.

William now had fourteen fugitives on his hands, more than his house could hold. Finding safe hiding places for everyone took time, and William didn't have the opportunity to write down all their stories. He did, however, record the story of the "hams" from Joseph Bustill.

Charles Bird, one of the group, had belonged to a farmer in Hagerstown. His owner wasn't especially cruel, but Charles resented the injustice of slavery. He worked without pay, risked flogging at any time, and could be sold to another owner whenever his master pleased.

The other runaways, George Dorsey, George's sister Angeline, Angeline's two sons, and another woman named Jane Scott, belonged to the wealthy owner of a milling business. All of them despised their master. He was a stern man, difficult to satisfy and quick to threaten them with the auction block.

Charles and George had planned the group's get-away. Hagerstown was located just below the Pennsylvania border. They intended to cross into Pennsylvania and head northeast to Harrisburg. In Harrisburg, they had been told, they could find assistance from the Underground Railroad.

On a dark spring night, Charles and George helped themselves to a wagon and a pair of horses. With the two women and Angeline's sons on board, they set off. About nine miles up the road, two white men appeared out of the darkness. The white men took hold of the horses' reins, explaining that their carriage had broken down. They clearly expected the black people to get out and let them have the use of the wagon and horses.

The white men were in for a surprise. Charles and George had brought along clubs and were willing to use them. In the struggle that followed, the wagon was overturned and the white men knocked unconscious. Now the fugitives' situation had turned desperate. If they were caught at this point, they would face terrible penalties for attacking white men. But the wagon in which they had planned to escape was no longer usable.

Charles and George made a quick decision. They rapidly unhitched the horses and set off bareback with each horse carrying three people. Some forty miles up the road they abandoned the exhausted animals. By now, they had entered Pennsylvania, but they knew no one they could turn to for help. They spent the next week struggling on foot over hills and through woods. Finally they crossed the Susquehanna River and entered Harrisburg. There they found Joseph Bustill.

William Still felt sure the loss of six slaves had caused a great commotion around Hagerstown— to say nothing of a missing wagon, two stolen horses, and a pair of injured white men! One of the angry slave owners must have contacted a paid informant in Harrisburg who advised him that the fugitives had passed through that city and were now headed for Philadelphia. The owner sent the telegram to the police officer believing that the officer would capture the runaways, and the rights of Maryland slave owners would triumph.

Instead, all six fugitives had vanished. The "hams" were safe in Philadelphia, and slavery had been dealt another blow.

❧ ❧ ❧

Joseph Cassey Bustill, the person who sent William Still the coded telegraph, was a free black man and a school teacher. Bustill took pleasure in outwitting slaveholders. On one occasion, he played a trick on a Maryland slave owner who had come to Harrisburg in search of eight runaway slaves. Someone had told him Bustill might be able to help. Bustill directed the man to return to Maryland and come back to Harrisburg in a couple of weeks. By then, he said, he might have information.

Actually, Bustill had already forwarded those fugitives to Philadelphia and knew that William Still had sent them north. But Bustill was delighted to make the slave owner waste time and money traveling back and forth. Bustill wrote to William Still: "I intend to make him spend a few more dollars, and if possible get a little sicker of this bad job." He hoped William could send him some letters written by the fugitives from their new location, letters that would make it clear to the owner that his slaves were free and happy. "Do try and send him a few bitter pills for his weak nerves and disturbed mind," Bustill urged gleefully.

CHAPTER 17

FIFTEEN IN CAPTAIN B.'S SCHOONER

Fear of Yellow Fever
July 1856

In the 1820s a fourteen-mile canal was constructed between the north end of the Chesapeake Bay and the south end of the Delaware River. After that, most boats leaving Baltimore, Norfolk, and Richmond took the shorter route to Philadelphia. Some were sailing boats called schooners that carried cargoes of cord wood, shingles, corn, oysters, fish, whiskey, and turpentine. Sometimes the schooners brought human cargo as well.

One seaman willing to transport runaway slaves was a man William Still referred to as Captain B. Captain B. charged for his services and made no secret of the fact. Well aware of the risk the captain was taking, fugitives willingly paid him fares that ranged from $25 to $100. On this trip the fugitives' fierce determination and the captain's cool manner were

both needed to bring them through a dangerous voyage.

ᴈ ᴈ ᴈ

The disappearance of a single slave angered
Southern slave owners. When fifteen escaped at
once, slave owners in the Norfolk area must
have been furious. Fifteen men, women, and children had simply vanished—and they all reached
Philadelphia safely.

William Still often asked fugitives why they
decided to run away. In addition to the desire
for freedom, many mentioned cruel owners and
the threat of being sold South. Sometimes other
motives contributed to the decision as well. Among
the group from Norfolk were four women who had
their own special reasons.

Sophia Gray wanted her children to grow
up free. Her son and daughter were mulattoes—
people with both black and white ancestors. Maybe
Sophia's white owner was the father of her children. That wasn't uncommon during slavery times.
Whatever the explanation, Sophia knew that her
children's mixed racial heritage wouldn't save them
from a hard life as slaves so Sophia decided to save
the children herself by taking them away on the
Underground Railroad.

Unlike Sophia, Sarah Saunders had no children.
Young and pretty, she hadn't even considered running away until she was approached in Norfolk by
an Underground Railroad agent. The agent knew
Sarah's sister, who lived in Philadelphia. He asked

if Sarah would like to see her sister again. When Sarah said yes, the agent told her that he could arrange passage on the Underground Railroad. Sarah eagerly accepted.

Rebecca Lewey went north because her husband sent her. Like his wife, Henry Lewey was a slave. He was also an experienced manager of the Underground Railroad in Norfolk. Lately, Henry had had reason to believe that slave owners were growing suspicious of his activities. It was time for Henry and his wife to take their own trip north on the Underground Railroad. Henry decided that Rebecca should go first to get her out of danger. He intended to follow as soon as he could.

The fourth woman was Mrs. Walker. Mrs. Walker was convinced that God hadn't meant her to be a slave, so she decided to set things right by running away. Mrs. Walker weighed two hundred and sixty pounds, enough to make two ordinary-sized women. Her ample size would cause problems on the passage north.

Someone had asked Captain B. if he would smuggle these women and eleven other runaway slaves to Philadelphia, and the captain agreed. On an evening in early July, the slaves gathered at a hidden spot on a river bank. They waited in the gathering darkness for the small oyster boat that was supposed to row them out to Captain B.'s schooner. Suddenly they heard a noise. Were the local watchmen approaching? They had to hide!

On the opposite bank, a wooden cradle held a boat awaiting repairs. The fugitives waded through the shallow water and crouched, soaking wet, in the dense shadows behind the boat.

Minutes ticked by, and no watchman appeared. Finally, about ten o'clock, the oyster boat arrived. The boatman ferried the fugitives out to the schooner, and Captain B., his young son, and the ship's mate helped them on board.

Beneath the schooner deck was a cleverly constructed hiding place large enough to hold human cargo—but the opening that led down was too small for hefty Mrs. Walker to squeeze through. Reluctantly, the captain decided that Mrs. Walker could remain on deck, concealed in a cabin behind a load of corn the schooner was transporting.

When the other fugitives were stowed away, the schooner started up the Chesapeake Bay. For fifteen hours, the passengers sat crowded together in their cramped hiding place, barely able to breathe. Finally Captain B. let them come up for air, but he told them that they couldn't stay on deck for long. The schooner was approaching the canal that connected the bay to the Delaware River. As the boat passed through the canal locks, canal employees might see them. The fugitives had to return to their hiding place, and Captain B. told Mrs. Walker that now she must go down as well.

Mrs. Walker wanted to obey, but hard as she tried the poor woman could not wedge her ample body through the small opening. Her worried companions insisted that she must succeed. If she was discovered, her presence could betray them all. Mrs. Walker made another effort, but she simply could not fit through.

The situation seemed hopeless. Then one of the women said firmly that Mrs. Walker had to take off her clothes. Mrs. Walker didn't hesitate. If that was the price of freedom, she would pay it. She removed her dress and her thick layers of petticoats. With people pushing from above and people tugging from below, Mrs. Walker, scraped and bruised, squeezed through the hole.

If the hiding place had been crowded before, the situation was far worse now as hefty Mrs. Walker settled herself into that cramped space with the other fugitives. They had been traveling since the previous night, jostled by the pitching of the boat, breathing in the heavy odors of tar, turpentine and their own sweat. Coated with grime, they surely ached with fatigue as well. But no one complained. They simply pushed closer together to fit everyone in.

With the fugitives safely stowed, Captain B. stretched a tight-fitting oil-cloth across the opening in the deck and set a heavy table on top. No sign of the secret space was visible now, no indication that the schooner might be transporting secret cargo.

But at the first lock, a dangerous situation developed. Three officers boarded the boat to make an official inspection. They said that they had received a telegram from Norfolk informing them that this boat might contain runaway slaves. The officers questioned the captain's young son, the ship's mate, and Captain B., but no one gave away any hint of the illegal cargo stored on the boat.

When Captain B. was interviewed, he asked casually whether the officers had heard that yellow fever was raging in Norfolk. There was no fever in Norfolk, but the officers didn't know that. They did know, however, that Captain B.'s schooner had set out from that city. He and his crew might be infected with the deadly disease! The officers immediately ended their questioning and began a hasty search of the schooner.

Below deck, the frightened fugitives could hear the officers moving around. No one made a sound as footsteps thudded above them and gruff voices rose and fell. They knew that, at any moment, the trap door might fling open, and an angry voice could order them out.

The officers finished examining the upper deck and began taking up the hatchways to the hold. Foul air spilled out, and the officers jumped back. One officer swore the air carried the stench of yellow fever. Captain B. simply shrugged and told them to search to their hearts' content.

But the officers had had enough. They declared officially that there were no slaves on the boat, collected the three-dollar search fee, and released the schooner. Soon Captain B. was guiding his vessel out of the canal into the Delaware River.

Night was falling as they approached the city of Philadelphia. Captain B. knew he couldn't unload his illegal cargo at the city wharves. Instead, he planned to dock at League Island on the southern edge of the city, where the Schuylkill River emptied into the Delaware.

Earlier, the captain had sent a message to William Still advising him of the plan and asking him to meet the schooner. Aware of the large number of passengers on board, William had hired three carriages and three trustworthy drivers. Between ten and eleven that night, they drove to the appointed meeting place.

The riverside was quiet as a country graveyard. By the pale light of the moon, William made out a mast. As they drew closer to the water, he saw Captain B.'s schooner anchored below a steep embankment. In the shadows on the deck, fifteen fugitives waited, eager to step off onto free soil. The moment was electric with excitement, but silence was essential. Only whispers could be exchanged.

From the top of the river bank, William Still and his helpers pulled the fugitives, one by one, up the incline. When it was Mrs. Walker's turn, she eagerly stretched out her arms. The waiting helpers caught hold of her hands and pulled as hard as they could, but they couldn't budge the hefty woman.

The captain watched, laughing at their struggle. Finally he joined the effort. With the captain heaving from behind and William and his helpers pulling from in front, Mrs. Walker struggled to the top. She was a free woman at last, as she believed God had meant her to be.

The Norfolk fugitives reached Philadelphia around the Fourth of July, a festive holiday in the city where the Declaration of Independence was signed. While Philadelphians were celebrating the 80th anniversary of the nation's independence, the fugitives celebrated their own independence. Slaves no longer, they were free people at last—almost. Their journey wasn't quite over.

With financial aid from the Vigilance Committee and arrangements made by William Still, they continued north. Some settled in New Bedford, Massachusetts, believing they would be safe there. Others crossed the border into Canada, where their freedom was assured.

Rebecca Lewey chose Canada and her story had a happy postscript. A few months after she settled there, her husband Henry escaped from Norfolk and joined her.

ﷺ ﷺ ﷺ

In June 1858, two years after that trip to Philadelphia, runaway slaves were discovered on board Captain B.'s schooner, and he was taken prisoner in Virginia. William Still gave no further information regarding Captain B.'s fate, but he was probably treated harshly. Six months earlier, another seaman had brought five fugitives from Norfolk in a skiff, and his role in the escape was discovered. For the crime of helping slaves find freedom, that unfortunate man was convicted and sentenced to twenty-five years in Richmond Penitentiary where he died during the Civil War.

CHAPTER 18

LEAR GREEN

Stowed in a Sailor's Chest
May 1857

In March 1857, the United States Supreme Court ruled on a case involving a suit brought by a slave named Dred Scott. The court decided that black people weren't citizens, and therefore Dred Scott had no legal right to establish a suit in any United States court. Chief Justice Roger B. Taney wrote the majority ruling. The ruling stated that the men who wrote the Constitution didn't believe that blacks had any rights that white people were bound to respect. A black person could be bought, sold, and treated in every way like any other article of merchandise.

Slaveholders were delighted with that ruling while white Northerners who opposed slavery reacted with anger. It's hard to imagine the pain and outrage felt by black people. As a young slave in Baltimore, Lear Green surely heard about the Dred Scott decision. Perhaps it helped convince her to attempt the daring escape described in the following narrative.

ஃ ஃ ஃ

Imagine a seaman's chest the size of a trunk. Picture a young woman climbing into the chest and huddling down in the cramped space inside. The lid closes with a thud, sealing the young woman in darkness. Someone winds a rope around the chest. Now she is totally trapped. Without help, she can't get out.

Could you survive eighteen hours curled up in that narrow space and stifling darkness? Lear Green did. She endured that terrifying experience because of her fierce desire for freedom. Eighteen-year-old Lear wanted to marry, and she was determined not to enter marriage as a slave.

Lear belonged to a butter dealer in Baltimore. The butter dealer had inherited Lear from his mother-in-law. That was how slavery worked. The woman had given the little girl to her son-in-law the same way she would have willed him a pocket watch or a pair of leather boots. Lear's next mistress was the wife of the man who inherited her. This mistress was stern and harsh, quick to set one task after another for the child and quick to find fault with the way she did those tasks.

By age eighteen, Lear had grown into a modest, graceful young woman—and she had fallen in love. The man who had won her heart was a free black man named William Adams, a skilled barber who also worked at local taverns, opening oysters.

William asked Lear to marry him, but Lear didn't believe she could be a good wife while she was owned by another man. Moreover, she couldn't bear the idea that their children, born to a slave mother, would automatically be slaves as well. Lear made up her mind to find freedom.

She and William Adams considered many possibilities. At last, they decided on a risky plan. William would leave Baltimore and travel to the city of Elmira in northern New York. Lear would follow later, shipped to Philadelphia inside a seaman's chest and continuing north from there. William's mother, a free black person like her son, had friends in Philadelphia and would accompany the chest on its dangerous journey.

A suitable chest was obtained, and a pillow and quilt, some clothes, a little food, and a bottle of water were gathered in preparation for the trip. William set off for Elmira weighed down by concern for his sweetheart. A few days later, Lear climbed inside the chest with her supplies, ready to endure whatever lay ahead.

The chest was taken to the wharf and placed on board a steamer bound for Philadelphia. The chest, like other cargo, was stowed on the open deck. Black passengers had to ride outside with the cargo, but that suited William's mother. She wanted to be as close to Lear as possible.

During the night the steamer moved steadily up the Chesapeake Bay. William's mother waited until no one was around. Quietly she untied the ropes that bound the chest and lifted the lid a little. No words were spoken, but that brief, silent contact reassured her that Lear was alive. Lear, closed inside the stifling space of the chest, must have welcomed those few minutes when she could breathe cool salt air.

After eighteen weary hours, the steamer docked in Philadelphia. The chest was delivered to the home where William Adams' mother would be staying. Frantic with worry, the mother and her friends removed the ropes and raised the lid. Lear was unharmed. Stiff and weary from her hard journey, she stepped out of the chest to breathe the exhilarating air of freedom.

Lear undoubtedly received a joyful welcome, but she couldn't stay long in that house. Back in Maryland, her furious owner was already advertising Lear's escape in *The Baltimore Sun*. The ad included a description of the missing slave and said that she had probably been "persuaded off" by a Negro man named William Adams who had disappeared from Baltimore a week earlier. The ad contained a drawing of a black woman in a long dress running along on foot. A far cry from the way Lear had traveled!

Lear's owner offered a reward of $50 if the fugitive was captured in Maryland, $150 if she was brought back from another state. Slave catchers in Philadelphia would undoubtedly take note of that ad and be on the lookout for a young woman answering Lear's description. A stranger staying in the house where William Adams' mother was a guest would surely draw attention. Lear had to be hidden elsewhere.

The Vigilance Committee offered to help. Lear and the seaman's chest were moved to William Still's house. She stayed there for several days while William made arrangements to send her north.

Lear reached Elmira safely and found her sweetheart waiting. She and William Adams were married and settled in Elmira. Sadly, the joys of marriage and the loving family life Lear had struggled to attain didn't last long—Lear Green Adams died just three years later.

ᱛᱛ ᱛᱛ ᱛᱛ

William Still wanted people to understand the enormous risk Lear had taken. Before she left Philadelphia, he had a photo taken showing Lear kneeling inside the sailor's chest. That image still exists. Face calm, eyes steady, Lear looks out from the open chest, reminding all who see the photo of the young woman's willingness to face any ordeal in order to win her freedom.

CHAPTER 19

JOHN BROWN

Attack at Harpers Ferry
October 1859

John Brown had a plan to end slavery. The fiery abolitionist planned to raid the federal arsenal in Harpers Ferry, Virginia. He intended to seize the guns stored in the arsenal and arm area slaves. He expected other slaves to join the revolt. Eventually, he believed, slavery would collapse.

It didn't turn out that way. Within thirty-six hours of the attack on the arsenal, most of Brown's band of twenty-one men had been killed or captured. Brown himself had been wounded and taken prisoner.

News of the attack swept the country like a firestorm. Supporters of slavery directed their fury at abolitionists. It was a dangerous time, and William Still had special cause for concern. William was acquainted with John Brown and some of his followers. He had been told of Brown's plan but thought the idea was unworkable and would end in disaster. William had no idea that Brown intended to go ahead until news of the attack reached Philadelphia.

Newspapers began publishing letters and other documents found with Brown's men. One memo said: "Wrote William Still Wednesday." William was afraid that note would lead authorities to his door. The authorities didn't show up, but two of John Brown's men did. They had escaped from Harpers Ferry, and each had found his way to Philadelphia, ragged, footsore, hungry, and in desperate need of help. Their presence endangered William and his family, but William dealt with the situation in his usual cool-headed way. With his help, both men escaped to Canada.

John Brown's wife also stayed with the Stills during her husband's trial for treason in Charles Town, Virginia. John Brown was found guilty and hanged on December 2, 1859, but the furious outcry provoked by the attack on Harpers Ferry went on. As violence against abolitionists grew more intense, William feared his records would be discovered. He had to find a new hiding place.

After much thought, William moved his notebooks and other papers to a black burial ground called Lebanon Cemetery. Stored in the loft of the cemetery building amid dust and cobwebs, William hoped those records would be safe from discovery.

CHAPTER
20

HARRIET TUBMAN AND THE ENNETS FAMILY

Guarded by an Angel
December 1860

William Still often worked hand in hand with two of the best known members of the Underground Railroad: Harriet Tubman and Thomas Garrett.

Harriet Tubman was born into slavery on a plantation in Dorchester County, far down the Eastern Shore of Maryland. She ran away in 1849 and managed to reach Philadelphia. Not content merely to find her own freedom, she returned a year later and smuggled out her niece and the niece's two children. Over the next ten years, Harriet went back and forth nearly twenty times guiding slaves north. She rescued over 300 people, including many of her own relatives. Sometimes Harriet accompanied fugitives all the way up to Canada. Sometimes she led them to William Still in Philadelphia. Other times she stopped off in Wilmington,

Delaware, where she put the fugitives in the care of Thomas Garrett.

Thomas Garrett was a successful Quaker merchant in Wilmington, a few miles from the Pennsylvania border. He was also a highly active stationmaster on the Underground Railroad, in frequent contact with William Still. Garrett sent fugitives into Philadelphia in many different ways—on foot, hidden in a wagon, as passengers in the railway cars, traveling by steamboat. To outwit slave catchers, Garrett sometimes used a roundabout route that wound through Chester County, Pennsylvania. A number of Quakers in Chester County, including relatives of Thomas Garrett, assisted the Underground Railroad. These Quakers moved fugitives from house to house and farm to farm until it was safe to send them to William Still or put them on a train headed north.

The following story tells about the last time William and Thomas Garrett worked with Harriet Tubman to rescue a group of runaway slaves.

 ❧ ❧ ❧

One of the worst horrors of slavery was the way it tore families apart. On any day, without warning, a slave could be sold to a new owner. Wives were separated from husbands, children taken from parents, never to see each other again.

Stephen Ennets and his wife Maria understood this painful possibility well. Stephen and Maria belonged to different masters in Dorchester County, Maryland. Although they lived eight miles apart and could spend little time together, their love for each other and their children was strong.

Maria was hired out by her owner and paid him ten dollars a year for the privilege. With what she earned, she supported herself and the couple's children, two small daughters and a three-month-old baby. It was a fine arrangement for the slave owner. It cost him nothing to feed and clothe Maria and the children, and when the children were old enough, he could put them out to work as well.

Stephen and Maria worried constantly about the future. Growing up in slavery, their children would always live under the threat of sale and separation. Finally, the Ennets made up their minds. Despite the dangers involved, they would look for a way to escape.

Stephen and Maria had heard stories about a mysterious woman whom slaves called Moses. Silent as smoke, invisible as air, Moses slipped onto plantations in Dorchester County and spirited slaves north. Moses was Harriet Tubman. Like Moses in the Bible, Harriet led fugitives to the promised land of freedom. Slave owners in Dorchester County wanted desperately to capture Harriet Tubman. They had offered fat rewards that made slave catchers eager to snare her, but so far, Harriet had evaded all their efforts.

Stephen and Maria got word to Harriet Tubman, asking her to help them escape with their children. Another slave named John wanted to go along. Harriet agreed to take them all.

They knew the journey would be difficult.

It was December, a time of harsh weather, and Harriet would lead them much of the way on foot as she often did, slipping through woods, fields, and swamps, crisscrossing streams and rivers to throw off pursuers. The trip would be challenging for adults, even more so with three small children along. The presence of the children would also make it easier for anyone who spotted the group to recognize them as the missing runaways.

From the beginning, troubles slowed their progress. They left at night, Harriet carrying the baby in a basket, trudging through snow that gave way to icy rain. As dawn approached, Harriet hid her charges in the underbrush and approached a house she was familiar with. A black man lived there, a member of the Underground Railroad who had often provided her with assistance. But when Harriet gave the secret knock, a white man flung up the window and demanded to know who she was and what she wanted. Startled, Harriet asked about the person she knew. "Gone," snarled the white man. "Driven out for sheltering niggers."

Avoiding further questions, Harriet hurried off. She knew the man would report her visit to authorities, but she had no clear plan for where to hide now or how to move forward. The unexpected loss of this reliable Underground Railroad contact had thrown her off balance, a grim reminder that times had grown more perilous.

Then, as often happened in Harriet Tubman's life, an inner voice seemed to provide direction. She led the Ennets and John into a nearby marsh where they waded through muddy water and tall grass to a small island. Harriet told them to lie down , and they obeyed. All day, chilled through, they lay on the damp ground.

As dusk thickened, they heard a voice. Peering through the dense grass, Harriet saw a white man in Quaker garb walking along the edge of the marsh. The man was alone, but he spoke loud enough for Harriet to hear the curious statements that came from his mouth. The man said that his wagon stood in the barnyard of the nearest farm. His horse waited inside the stable, and the harness hung on the wall. The man repeated the same information several times. Then he went away.

Harriet had heard the message. When the night was fully dark, she crept to the nearby farm and returned with the horse and wagon. She loaded the weary fugitives aboard and urged the horse forward, headed for another Quaker farm some distance away. The farmer promised to return the borrowed horse and wagon, and Harriet and her companions set off once more on foot, never knowing how the mysterious Quaker had learned of their plight and their location in the swamp.

With fear of discovery greater than ever, they made halting progress. About thirty miles below Wilmington, Harriet left Maria and the children in a safe location. Perhaps the children were exhausted, or perhaps Harriet felt it was safer now to split up. She could travel quickly to Wilmington with Stephen and John, then return to collect Maria and the children.

Just outside Wilmington, Harriet and the men entered the tiny town of New Castle. Harriet found a hiding place there for Stephen and John, then continued into Wilmington to confer with Thomas Garrett.

Harriet and Thomas Garrett worked out plans for the next part of the journey. Garrett would take responsibility for Stephen and John. He would pay a man he trusted to go to New Castle and escort the two fugitives across the state line into Chester County. From there, other Underground Railroad agents would arrange for them to reach Philadelphia.

Meanwhile, Harriet would return to Maria and the children. Harriet told Thomas Garrett that she knew a man with a carriage who would convey them to the same Chester County location Stephen and John were heading for. Garrett agreed to that arrangement and gave Harriet ten dollars to pay for the carriage.

But Garrett was worried. Writing to William Still to explain the plans, Garrett said: "I shall be very uneasy about them, till I hear they are safe." Garrett had recently learned disturbing news. Slave-catchers were keeping a lookout on the two roads that led into Chester County. The carriage bearing Maria and the children would have to travel one or other of those roads, and Garrett feared they were headed into a trap. Nevertheless, Garrett's letter ended on an optimistic note: " . . . as it is Harriet, who seems to have had a special angel to guard her on her journey of mercy, I have hope."

That special angel—perhaps the same angel that had earlier sent the horse and wagon—watched over Harriet again. She arrived safely in Philadelphia along with the Ennets family and John, and the Vigilance Committee received them warmly. In his book William wrote: "They were cheered with clothing, food, and material aid, and sped on to Canada."

The journey wasn't over yet, but thanks to Moses and the Underground Railroad, Stephen and Maria Ennets would finally receive their wish—their children could grow up free.

&a &a &a

Maryland slaveholders, enraged by Harriet's continual success in spiriting fugitives to freedom, raised the bounty for her capture to the staggering sum of $40,000. In addition, they discussed cruel devices that could be used to torture her and put her to death. The situation in Dorchester County had finally grown too dangerous for Harriet Tubman. The journey that freed the Ennets family was Moses' final trip to Maryland.

CHAPTER
21

CIVIL WAR

A Country Divided
1861 to 1865

In November 1860, one month before Harriet Tubman had to abandon her trips to Maryland, the deeply divided nation had elected Abraham Lincoln president. For the South, any further compromise over slavery was now impossible. South Carolina withdrew from the Union, and other Southern states followed.

In Philadelphia, Lincoln wasn't popular. Abolitionists were few in number and widely despised while support for the South continued strong. Then, in February 1861, something significant happened.

On his way to Washington to be sworn into office, President-elect Lincoln visited several northern cities, including Philadelphia. Lincoln arrived during the celebration of George Washington's birthday. Addressing a crowd at Independence Hall, Lincoln said that he had often asked himself what great principle held the states together. He had concluded that the principle unifying our nation sprang from the Declaration of Independence, which gave liberty to Americans and the hope of liberty to the world. The Declaration had promised, said Lincoln, that "in due time the weights should be lifted from the shoulders of all men, and that all should have an equal chance."

On other days, at other locations, many Philadelphians would have booed any statement Lincoln made that suggested putting an end to slavery. But on this day celebrating George Washington in front of the building where the nation began, the crowd was caught up in the spirit of the event and their surroundings. The Philadelphia audience cheered Lincoln's speech, and the words Lincoln spoke and the applause he received signaled the beginning of a change in the city's mood.

Many Philadelphians continued to despise black people. Many still sympathized with the South. But Philadelphia was the nation's birthplace, the city where the Declaration of Independence and the Constitution had been created, and Philadelphians took great pride in that legacy. To defend it, they had to defend the Union—even if that meant supporting war with the South.

Lincoln was sworn in as president on March 4, 1861. On April 12, South Carolina fired on federal troops at Fort Sumter, and the long and terrible Civil War began. When it ended, the Union had survived, and slavery had been abolished.

The Underground Railroad never posed a major threat to slavery. Compared to the total population of enslaved people—almost four million just before the Civil War—only a small number of slaves escaped. But every fugitive who reached the north forced Northerners to face more clearly the truth about slavery. Southerners claimed that slaves were satisfied with their lives. The steady flow of fugitives running north proved that wasn't so. Southerners claimed that slaves couldn't care for themselves, but fugitives, once free, held jobs, bought property, and enjoyed self-sufficient lives.

The Underground Railroad didn't destroy slavery. It didn't even free many slaves. But it contributed to the complex chain of events that produced the Civil War, and the war ended slavery.

WILLIAM STILL'S BOOK

Honoring Heroes
1872

When William Still hid his record books and papers in the loft of the Lebanon Cemetery building in 1860, he didn't know when, if ever, it would be safe to bring that material to light again. He had no idea, at that time, that war would soon break out, and slavery would be washed away in the blood of Union and Confederate soldiers.

William's records stayed hidden until the conflict ended. Then, with danger past, William returned to Lebanon Cemetery. He climbed up to the dusty loft full of anxiety, wondering whether the records he had so carefully preserved were in ruins. Had mildew blotted the pages or mice shredded the paper for nests? To William's relief, his records had survived intact.

He carried them home, stored them away, and turned to other pressing concerns. William's life was different now. When the Civil War burst upon the nation, the work of the Anti-Slavery Society ended. The executive committee told William with regret that his services were no longer needed. After fourteen years in the anti-slavery office, William needed a different way to earn a living.

With typical initiative, William decided that he would start his own business. The Fifth Street building formerly occupied by the Anti-Slavery Society was now empty. William rented the property and moved his family into the upstairs rooms. On the ground floor he sold and repaired coal stoves.

Friends warned him that a business owned by a black man couldn't succeed in a city as prejudiced as Philadelphia. William proved them wrong. Customers were impressed by his work ethic, efficiency, and honesty, and his business did well. Based on that first success William built a coal yard, which also prospered.

Other interests also filled William's life. After slavery was abolished, unfair treatment of blacks had continued. In Philadelphia, black people had never been allowed to ride the horse-drawn cars that carried passengers around the city. William had begun to protest that policy in 1859 and didn't stop opposing it until the policy was overturned in 1867.

William worked to help the black community in other ways as well. He raised funds to assist former slaves, founded the Black Young Men's Christian Association, and served on the boards of homes for poor black children and elderly black people.

In May 1871, William was asked to take on another challenge. Members of the Anti-Slavery Society knew about William's records and recognized the importance of the information he had preserved. They passed a unanimous resolution urging William to publish an account of his work with the Underground Railroad.

The timing was difficult for William. By now he and Letitia had four children, and he was working hard to build his coal business. Besides, William had little formal education and no experience in publishing a book.

But he remembered the gripping accounts he had heard from fugitives describing their struggle toward freedom. Some had splashed through swamps, waded streams, walked till their shoes fell apart and their clothes turned into rags, and then crawled for shelter into a cave or hollow tree, always fearful when they fell asleep that they would wake to the sound of shouts and baying hounds. Many had gone for long periods without food or water until their stomachs felt hollow and their mouths were parched. Often they carried scars on their shoulders from whippings—and deeper scars in their hearts from losing family members.

After passing through Philadelphia, most of these fugitives had vanished off the pages of history. Only William, with his carefully preserved records, could tell the world what they had gone through. So he did.

William's book, *The Underground Railroad*, was published in 1872. Along with hundreds of accounts that William had heard from fugitives, he included letters, newspaper articles, and other material. The book was well received when first published and has been reprinted often. Today, it is recognized by historians as the most authentic source of information about the Eastern branch of the Underground Railroad. But the book isn't just for historians. The accounts of desperate escapes, undertaken by determined fugitives, remind us all that the desire for freedom often motivates ordinary people to act in heroic ways.

William Still died of heart disease in 1902. In his long, well-spent life, he had overcome poverty, lack of education, and prejudice. He had risked danger and possible imprisonment to help hundreds of runaway slaves find freedom—and he had saved their stories for the world in a remarkable book.

CHAPTER

AFTERWORD

About William Still's Book

William Still was a man who saved things. In addition to records relating to fugitives, he held onto letters, newspaper articles, accounts of court hearings, and notices offering rewards for the return of runaway slaves. When he was asked by the Anti-Slavery Society in 1871 to write a book about the Underground Railroad, Still had a wealth of material to draw on—and an enormous challenge to face.

William Still had no experience with book publishing. Moreover, he was by then the busy owner of a successful coal business; he also had numerous civic commitments and a wife and children to care for. Still realized, however, that his records were unique. After the Civil War, his original reason for saving the accounts of runaway slaves no longer mattered, but another reason for publishing them, equally important, had taken its place. These stories provided powerful insights into the dangers and hardships the fugitives had faced for the sake of liberty. William Still wanted their descendants—and all Americans—to know their stories.

When a strike occurred among Pennsylvania coal miners, William Still decided to use the lull in business activity to attempt the huge task. Working from five in the morning till eleven at night, Still spent seven months compiling the manuscript for an 800-page book. He hired engravers to create illustrations and entered into an agreement with the Philadelphia firm of Porter & Coates to publish the book.

The publisher's handwritten contract promised that *The Underground Railroad* would be "gotten up in first-class style," available in four different bindings at prices ranging from $4.50 to $6.50. Sales were to be made by subscription, and Still would receive a royalty of 62½ cents for each copy sold.

William Still may have lacked experience in publishing, but he was a smart businessman. He formed teams of black salespersons to travel around the country, soliciting orders. Advance copies of the book were sent to major newspapers and prominent individuals, and Still included their favorable comments in his advertising brochures. The first printing of *The Underground Railroad* sold out, then the second. For the third printing, Still took on the role of publisher, realizing that it was more profitable for him to produce the book on his own.

In 1876 Philadelphia marked the 100th birthday of the United States with a huge Centennial Exhibition celebrating American achievements. William Still arranged for copies of *The Underground Railroad* to be included in the exhibition. The display was good publicity, of course, but Still also wanted people to know that black Americans were capable of writing and publishing a major book.

After Still's death in 1902, *The Underground Railroad* was reprinted several more times and is now considered an American classic. However, his sprawling book is more admired than read. Still's text is hard to follow and often confusing. The book has no clear pattern of organization, and different kinds of material—letters, newspaper articles, legal documents, minutes of anti-slavery meetings—are interwoven with fugitive records. Many of the individual records Still included provide little more than the fugitives' names, the names of their owners, and the locations where they were held in bondage. Dramatic escape stories are also there, buried among other accounts, but they are often incomplete and erratic in time sequence.

These shortcomings in William Still's book are hardly surprising. It was a complicated job for Still to sort through the mass of documents he had saved, many handwritten. Still had no secretary to help organize the material and no editor to help him refine the manuscript he produced. And, of course, he had to create his lengthy book without the aid of a computer or even an old-fashioned manual typewriter.

The amazing thing is that Still completed this book at all. Despite its shortcomings, the striking assets of *The Underground Railroad* stand out—the authentic power of the information it provides and the spotlight the book beams on so many heroic fugitives and the people who helped them along the way.

Author's Note

Descendants of the Still family live today in New Jersey near the place where Levin and Charity owned their farm, and family members hold regular reunions celebrating their rich heritage. I first learned about William Still some years ago when I read a news story concerning those reunions.

Until then, I'd never heard of William Still and knew nothing about the Underground Railroad in Philadelphia. When I realized that Still had published a book on that subject, I bought a copy, expecting to find the pages filled with exciting escapes of runaway slaves. But I quickly discovered the problems that keep most people from reading *The Underground Railroad*. There were marvelous stories hidden inside the confusing text, but only a determined reader would find them. Convinced that these accounts should reach a wider audience, I decided to write a book retelling some of Still's stories.

In choosing accounts to include, I looked for interesting escapes detailed enough to form the basis for a complete narrative. I selected stories that spanned the years of Still's involvement with the

Underground Railroad up to the outbreak of the Civil War. To provide historical context, I decided to include information about some of the complicated political events that form the backdrop of this troubled period.

Regarding the fugitives, my primary source of information was Still's book, the reprint edition published by the Johnson Publishing Company in 1970. In some cases Still's book is the only available source—if William Still had not kept his records, the painful lives and daring escapes of many of these people would have been lost to history. In other instances, additional research enabled me to fill in gaps and provide further information about the fugitives and the individuals who helped them. For a full list of sources I used, see the bibliography located with this book on the publisher's web site: www.townsendpress.com.

No major biography of William Still has yet been written, an omission I hope some historian will soon resolve. I found information about Still's family and later life in a biographical essay written by James P. Boyd and included in the third printing of *The Underground Railroad*, which Still himself published in 1886. All direct quotations come from Still's book or Boyd's essay.

While gathering information, I visited many sites that figure in Still's records and felt the presence of people he wrote about. Beside the canal that links the Chesapeake Bay and Delaware River, I recalled the fifteen fugitives huddled in determined silence below the deck of Captain B.'s schooner while, overhead, officials hunted for their hiding place. Along the Eastern Shore of Maryland, I pictured the Ennets family splashing through creeks and salt marshes, following Harriet Tubman out of bondage to the light of freedom. At Old Point Comfort, I thought of Charles Gilbert snatching up a woman's dress and bonnet in a last, desperate effort to fool the soldier who had come to seize him. Walking the streets of Norfolk, Richmond, Washington, and Baltimore, I reflected on the many black people bound in slavery in and around those cities who dreamed so hard of liberty that they risked their lives to find it.

The most powerful experience I had occurred with a visit to Independence Hall in Philadelphia. William Still passed by that building often on his way to the nearby Anti-Slavery Society office. On a few occasions, he went inside and climbed to the long room on the second floor once used as a federal courtroom. Standing in that same room, I remembered that Still had come here to attend the trials involving Euphemia Williams and Jane Johnson. In this building that so vividly symbolizes American freedom, William Still heard Southern lawyers argue that these two Americans had no claim to freedom—they were slaves, the property of white owners.

The lawyers lost, the women went free, and slavery soon ended. Since then, our country has made long strides toward equality for all its citizens, but the troubled past of Independence Hall reminded me that our liberty can never be taken for granted.

Writing this book has been both a challenge and an adventure. I am grateful to the Still family for the reunions that started me on my quest and for their determination to preserve and celebrate their family history. Early in my research, I had the good fortune to meet Phil Lapsansky, reference librarian at The Library Company of Philadelphia and an authority on William Still. Mr. Lapsansky generously provided information, suggestions for additional sources, and much valued encouragement. Through this long process, my husband has been endlessly patient and supportive in ways too numerous to count. I owe thanks also to John Langan, president of Townsend Press, for his conviction that these stories are valuable and for his commitment to making them available to a wider audience.

Most of all I feel gratitude to William Still. Often I felt overwhelmed by the task I had set myself. Then I would recall Still, scribbling furiously late at night, filling page after page with painful stories the fugitives told him and, years later, grappling with this mass of material, determined to shape it into a book that would honor their courage and preserve for the future an account of their journey to freedom. Remembering William Still's persistence, I always returned to work with fresh energy and renewed determination.

Source notes and bibliography can be found on the publisher's website, **www.townsendpress.com**, at the entry for *William Still and the Underground Railroad*.